MODERN ASCENSION

STORIES FROM THE SPIRITUAL PATHS OF HIGH INITIATES

COMPILED BY
CAROL ANNE HALSTEAD

FriesenPress

Suite 300 - 990 Fort St
Victoria, BC, V8V 3K2
Canada

www.friesenpress.com

Copyright © 2019 by Carol Anne Halstead

First Edition — 2019

All rights reserved.

No part of this publication may be reproduced in any form, or by any means, electronic or mechanical, including photocopying, recording, or any information browsing, storage, or retrieval system, without permission in writing from FriesenPress.

ISBN

978-1-5255-5433-9 (Hardcover)
978-1-5255-5434-6 (Paperback)
978-1-5255-5435-3 (eBook)

1. BODY, MIND & SPIRIT, HEALING, PRAYER & SPIRITUAL

Distributed to the trade by The Ingram Book Company

This book is dedicated to Verna Maruata and Waireti; in gratitude, for their commitment to their own Ascension and to the Ascension of all those who seek their guidance.

Table of Contents

Preface ix

Glossary of Terms. xix

Chapter One 1
    Carol Anne Halstead
    Finding the Flow

Chapter Two 10
    Elizabeth Tackenberg
    A Stirring in My Heart

Chapter Three 23
    Kathryn Murray
    Inner Reflections: Paths to Ascension

Chapter Four 34
    Elaine Marie
    My Blue Flame Heart: Primal Love

Chapter Five. 52
    AmayahGrace
    My Spiritual Journey…from four to seventy-four…(and counting!)

Chapter Six 63
    Brad Panopoulos
    A Journey Led by My Higher Self

Chapter Seven 73
    Geri Mason
    Over the Rainbow

Chapter Eight 83
   Simi Ahuja, M.D.
   A Trail of Love

Chapter Nine 96
   Luz Victoria Winter
   From Caterpillar to Butterfly

Chapter Ten 106
   Tammy Manzo
   My Ascension Lifetime

Chapter Eleven 121
   Sheila Franzen
   Unwavering Faith

Chapter Twelve 139
   Andrew Logan
   The Benevolent Universe

Chapter Thirteen 146
   Verna Maruata
   My Perfect Path

Conclusion 160

Preface

I grew up with the premise that God is external to us, and through good behaviour, following the sacraments as well as practicing devotion to Him, I could redeem myself sufficiently to move on to a happy afterlife as an eternal reward. There was no talk about God *within* because the idea that a human being could be worthy enough to be in the same league as an unknowable God was unthinkable. I accepted this teaching on faith.

However, as an adult in my early thirties in the 1980's, my religious views came into question when I began to explore the world of energy healing. As a nurse trained within the traditional medical model, I was blown away by the extraordinary healing that I was witnessing, and I really wanted to explore this new domain. I discovered that a new paradigm of healing was very slowly entering mainstream thinking. At the same time, there was more information becoming available about Eastern religions and the concept of enlightenment and spiritual awakening. I wanted to know so much more, not just about the nature of healing but also about spiritual knowledge.

I became a seeker. As I began to explore these new ideas, I immersed myself in the study of various healing modalities. I attended lectures by rising Western teachers, like Deepak Chopra, Wayne Dyer, Gary Zukav, and Eckhart Tolle, to name a few. I often watched Oprah to see who she was interviewing, so I could gain fresh insights. I accumulated books, tools, and experiences. I was learning and expanding my knowledge base about all things spiritual and healing.

It was an exciting time for me. Still, I began to question more deeply the purpose of these pursuits. I wanted to forge a clear path to spiritual growth and really focus on this aspect of my learning.

Fortunately, I was introduced to the notion of Ascension as a modern concept about a decade ago. The term Ascension was both new and old to my vocabulary. Through my religion, I had understood the term to mean what Jesus experienced following his resurrection. That is, Jesus "ascended into heaven and is seated at the right hand of the Father". From The Apostles' Creed – a Catholic prayer. I have since learned another definition of Ascension.

I've also learned that it is something that is available to everyone.

What is Ascension?

Ascension is a term used to describe the process by which an individual actively evolves into higher consciousness. Higher consciousness is an expanded state of awareness, which transcends beliefs.

Ascension is not something that will happen to us on a certain day or time, nor will we be part of a wave of people who will leave the earth all at once. Rather, it is what a person will experience as they grow in spiritual vibration. This vibration is increased by the greater Light and Radiance that comes into our chakras when we pay karma. Ascension is a vast spiritual process that does not appear to have an end point.

The reason we are focusing on it here is because there is a very important part of Ascension that everyone on earth can eventually accomplish. That is, with dedication and effort, everyone can clear their karma within their lifetimes—this means that you can leave the cycle of reincarnation. Karma is the negative thoughts, words, and actions that we have created in our past lives and in this life. All karma, past and present, is stored in our chakras. Anything unresolved from your previous lifetimes will be carried forward for clearing in this lifetime. Karma is created every day, when we think, do, or speak in ways that do not come from love. Thoughts, words and actions based on love, on the other hand, do not create karma. The only way to ascend is to clear the karma we have accumulated through many lifetimes. Once we do this, we no longer need to reincarnate.

Rebirth and reincarnation are concepts that are part of the ancient teachings of most Eastern religions. These teachings were expunged from Western doctrine during the sixth century, and because of this, Christianity has lost a fundamental understanding of the truth of our existence and has not recovered. Knowing about, and understanding the purpose of reincarnation is germane to understanding the process of Ascension.

When we reincarnate, we return to earth with a new identity without remembering our previous lives. We are "veiled" from our past life history and purpose, and so must begin again on a path to remembering. It is far too easy to get seduced or sidetracked by either the beauty or trauma we experience here as we go from lifetime to lifetime. However, once we accept the premise of the cycle of rebirth and its purpose, we can interrupt this need to come back here to earth with a new identity and without knowledge of our true purpose to guide us.

If you want to do this work, you are likely wondering how this can be accomplished without having to deny oneself a normal life, relationships, satisfying work, etc. There are multiple ways to achieve the clearing of karma in one's lifetime and the purging of the need to return to earth. Everyone who has contributed his or her story to this book has done this. Our spiritual paths and life journeys are unique.

We are all off the cycle of rebirth in human form, and our Ascension paths are moving forward now, often in service to humanity.

This is a gradual process. It used to take many lives of dedication to one's spirituality through sequestering to focus on devotion and meditation. Monasteries, nunneries, ashrams, or even caves were (and still are today) examples of where one could go to choose a life of devotion. However, in modern times, individuals do not need to live in an ashram or a cave and withdraw from ordinary life in order to achieve Ascension, and they can do so in a single lifetime. The term "householder," described first in *Autobiography of a Yogi* by Paramhansa Yogananda, refers to this process of climbing the Ascension ladder while in an ordinary—not secluded—life. This is today's modern method because it allows you to continue to participate in society where you can work to bring this higher consciousness to all your activities and interactions.

There are many paths to Ascension. For instance, there are Mystery Schools, some closed, some open, which provide a systematic approach to your spiritual growth. There is the Shamanic path that helps one to clear karma through visiting past lives and performing soul retrievals. There is the path of meditation from the Buddhist tradition. And there are also many other paths that have worked for others to achieve this spiritual goal.

What all of the storytellers in this book share in common is that, although we each arrived in this place at a different time and at a different pace, we have followed a systematic path, through initiations and used a variety of techniques intended to clear our karma. As you read these stories, you will see how each of us applied the same system and yet have had unique experiences. Still, we have all been successful at clearing our karma.

PREFACE

Whatever spiritual path you choose, I encourage you to always be discerning. It is essential to experience the freedom of choice when following someone's guidance. Even though this spiritual path can be hard work at times, if there is a perception of inner joy rather than fear throughout the process, then let this serve as your guide.

Why is Ascension so important?

As we ascend, we discover that there is an essential oneness in all of humanity; that is, we all came from one Source and we all have a spark of that divinity—Buddha Nature, Christ Self, Presence, or whatever you prefer to call it—which is the same within all of us. No matter what name you give it, this essence is common to us all. When we become aware of it and experience this rich truth, we can eventually come to recognize the "self in other," which naturally lessens one's inclination to hurt other sentient beings. Internalizing this notion can change how one goes about their business in the world. It can cause a ripple effect throughout one's relationships. It can influence the conduct of human affairs to move from what's good for the individual to what serves everyone. Ascension is not just a private event. It has the potential to impact our entire planet, galaxy, our universe, and the entire cosmos.

All of life stands to benefit from our efforts. While who we become and what we achieve is important, there is an even bigger job for us to individually accomplish while we are here on planet Earth. The truth is that we also have an inner purpose, and that inner purpose is the most important reason for our being here. That purpose is Ascension.

Why have all of us here chosen to ascend in this lifetime?

It must have been part of our souls' plan, because each of us have experienced varying degrees of attraction towards our own spiritual self-discovery journeys. The beauty of writing our stories for others to read lies in the uniqueness of these journeys. No two paths are the same. Yet we all share the same goal, which is to raise our spiritual vibration through clearing our karma and then to move past the cycle of reincarnation.

All of us storytellers here have found a more direct way to clear our karma. It is through our common association with Verna Maruata and Waireti. Through these two women, a group of Ascended Masters has created a portal in New Zealand, which was generated to help humanity in their Ascension. Unlike a natural vortex that emerges *from* Mother Earth, this portal was *brought down* to rest within Mother Earth for a short time.

Verna Maruata and Waireti are guardians for the portal. They work with the Ascended Masters on many levels, supporting their higher purpose. Through Verna Maruata, the Masters have gifted several techniques to help us in our Ascension and life paths, such as the Torus technique and the Perfect Path technique. Verna Maruata has two crown chakras, one for her and one for the Ascended Masters. Through this second crown chakra, the Masters send downloads of knowledge and understanding. Waireti has the gift of seeing energetically across dimensions and time. She sees the energetic realities. Waireti sees and Verna knows.

Together with the Masters, Verna Maruata and Waireti have developed a quantitative system for seeing and understanding Ascension in these modern times. This system of seeing and knowing has enabled them to bring people into the portal for practical healings that facilitate change and, in turn, facilitate Ascension.

Why read this book on Ascension?

The purpose of this book is to stimulate and encourage those who are looking for new understandings of spirituality and religion, and for those already on their seeker's journey to proceed along

PREFACE

their Ascension paths. It is my hope that this book will help you understand and accept why you should pursue Ascension and, most importantly, that you will find ways to clear your karma so that you can continue your soul's journey. You will become free to choose whether you wish to return to earth in another way—but it will be your choice. If you are reading this book, you are ready to do this work.

May this book inspire the desire and confidence in you that Ascension is something accomplishable, vitally important, and within your capacity. It is doable for you, just as it has been doable for us.

As you take a detailed look into the lives of thirteen spiritual aspirants who are actively ascending in different ways, you will find that you may even see yourself in parts of their stories. You will see what Ascension looks like in today's modern world. You will discover our varied outward paths. We are all quite different. We come from different parts of the world. We are young and old. Some are gifted healers and seers, some speak Light Language, some are employed in public work, and others are living quieter lives.

Yet there is one thing that we all have in common: Ascension. We have gone through each step, in sequence. You can't skip any parts of this journey.

In the past, the seeker's journey has required periods of isolation and deep meditation. Some of us have followed a spiritual teacher or guru. In fact, one of us—Luz Victoria Winter, spent years in India working directly with a guru. The spiritual growth she experienced was accelerated. She now lives and works in America with her family and continues to ascend. This was *her* perfect path. In a conversation I had with her some time ago, she suggested that perhaps, one day, someone should write about modern Ascension. In time, my Higher Self showed me an image of me sitting at a table with blank paper and a pen. Then, the title of this book came into my awareness: *Modern Ascension: Stories from the Spiritual Paths of High Initiates*. I felt a strong urge to post a request for participation on our Ascended Masters Facebook page. And the response was immediate: *Yes—I'm in!*

The beauty of reading our real-life stories is that they will show you that *you* can do this, too.

Ascension is for everyone.

Within this book, you will find thirteen stories in separate chapters, followed by a conclusion at the end. These stories have been placed in a specific energetic sequence to create a flow from story to story.

I applaud all these remarkable writers who have gone through the effort of digging deeply and describing their unique spiritual journeys here. For many of them, things have been changing quickly in their progression, even since the onset of their writing back in November of 2018. I appreciate their honesty, integrity, and ability to curate their own stories as things change for them. Moreover, I invited the storytellers in this book to show their authentic selves, which requires some vulnerability. This has not been an easy task for any of us. Self-exposure can invite judgement—but it is also an invitation to compassionate understanding of the life paths we have chosen.

For more information about some of the storytellers and high initiates in *Modern Ascension*, we welcome you to refer to the *Ascending Initiates* website at https://theascendinginitiates.com.

As some of the terms used in this book may be unfamiliar to you, there is a comprehensive glossary of essential terms included at the beginning of the book, which was written by Verna Maruata. Please refer to it for clarification along the way.

PREFACE

There are many sources of information about Ascension, karma, rays, and initiations, some of which are conflicting. The information you'll find in this book about these topics has been received by Verna Maruata and verified through Waireti's dimensional sight. The common language used throughout this book is from Verna's Ascended Masters website, which you can refer to at https://www.alphaimaging.co.nz .

In the next few years, there are going to be many more individuals who will start this journey of Ascension. It will change our world in profound ways. It has to. It is the most important purpose for our being here. Things are changing more quickly on our planet than ever before in recorded history. We have worldwide problems like climate crisis and poverty that need great commitment and creative problem solving to overcome.

It is time to take your spiritual yearning to the next step and to find your Ascension path. At some point in the foreseeable future, we will reach a tipping point with regard to Ascension. It will become an accepted fact that this is the purpose of our human experience. We are here in human physical form, but our deep inner purpose is to remember who we are in Spirit.

May your awakening journey be filled with love, joy, and inner peace, as well as the inner knowing of the profound support available to you as you follow your Ascension path.

My heartfelt thanks go to all who participated in bringing this book into being. The level of cooperation and commitment has astounded me.

Thank you to all the Elohim, Cosmic and Ascended Masters, Archangels, Devas, and Higher Selves for their never-ending support for all of us on earth who are on our Ascension journeys. Their assistance is only an ask away. This entire project has been supported by them, and has been over-lighted by Ganesh, a Cosmic Master.

Thank you to all the brave souls who said *yes* to this book, and for participating in the hard work of writing about their spiritual paths. They have all been humble and egoless and grateful to be able to tell their stories.

Thank you to Verna Maruata for her major contributions. Not just for her willingness to share her amazing story, but for writing the glossary as well. She readily provided assistance with definitions and content, as well as gave me important feedback on my writing. And thank you Waireti for the unseen support that I know was there.

I'd like to thank my "soul sisters", Jan Thompson and Barb Birdgeneau, (also seventh initiates), who supported this project from the outset, even helping me scour the bookshelves at our local Indigo bookstore for inspiring ideas for the book's cover. They provided helpful comments for my story and for the Preface. They are steadfast friends whom I cherish on this life's Ascension journey.

My good husband deserves heaps of credit for supporting me in all ways. I had tears when he said, after reading the Preface: "I want to read this book!" Those words of support meant everything to me.

Lastly, a hearty thank you to the brilliant folks at Friesen Press who have helped me bring this book to life.

I am grateful beyond words.

Carol Anne Halstead

April, 2019

Glossary of Terms

Akashic Records: A compendium of all the human events, words, thoughts, emotions, and intentions that have/will occur in the past, present and future. Many see the Akashic records as external, but a copy of each person's entire past-life history, karma, connections, patterns, and memories reside within one's individual soul seat and can be accessed via this energy center.

Ascended Master: A Being of Light (not in a body) who has left the cycle of rebirth by raising their vibration and consciousness to such a state that they have cleared all of their karma and dross from their chakras and bodies, thus attaining mastery over themselves. The Ascended Master is the Higher Self of the person who strived to ascend.

Ascended Masters Portal: For the Ascended Masters to be more effective in their support of humanity, they have constructed a vast portal in New Zealand. Unlike the natural portals found emerging from the Mother Earth (like in Sedona), this portal was constructed. One hundred and eight Ascended Masters, Cosmic Masters, Elohim, Archangels, and Devas slowly created their vast multi-dimensional portal over three years, bringing it down to anchor it within the Mother Earth. The portal assists the Masters in coming closer, to work with humanity in ways they have not been able to before. The portal allows vast Beings like the Cosmic Masters and Elohim to get closer to the vibration of humanity, while still protecting the integrity of the human form. The Masters have created this portal for their use, and their use alone.

Ascension: The process by which an individual actively evolves into an expanded state of awareness or higher consciousness.

Ascension vs Modern Ascension: The purpose of life is to ascend. This has been the focus of many gurus, monks, priests, and Holy men through the ages. Now, in these current times, Ascension is the focus not just for those that follow a religious path, but for those who follow a spiritual path. Ascension is now for the many, not for the few.

Ascension Master: The Ascended Master who walks with you to help you in your Ascension.

Chakras: A chakra is an energy center within the body. There are seven major chakras, many minor chakras, and seventy-two thousand minor energy points called nadis. The major chakras hold within them the karma we have yet to pay from past lives and from this life.

Double Crown Chakra: In the place of a crown chakra, Verna Maruata has two separate energy centers; one is hers, and the other is utilized by the Ascended Masters when she assists them with their work. This second center is rainbow coloured.

Dimensional Lives: We all exist as part of a collective of dimensional lives. Some of these dimensional lives are occurring concurrently with the life you are living now. Each of these lives is occurring in a dimension unique to them; for example, if you have nine dimensional lives, these lives are occurring in nine different dimensions. No one in this universe has the same dimensional collective as you—your dimensional collective is unique to you.

Dimensional lives are often erroneously thought to be lives of an individual replayed across dimensions. This is not so. Each dimensional life in your collective has a soul that is unique to them. Like you, their soul returns, life after life, to their own dimension for all of their lives. Each is a unique individual just as you are. They are separate from you. What makes you all part of a collective is that you all have the same Higher Self.

Grounding Oil: An oil created by a team of Ascended Masters that grounds all of your bodies (etheric, emotional, mental, and astral bodies) into the present. These oils are to be used daily and perpetually.

Higher Self: Your Higher Self is a Being on the path of Ascension. We all have a personal Higher Self. The Higher Self is the creator of your soul and the architect of your life and its lessons. You (the lower Self) are the vehicle for the Ascension of your Higher Self.

Holy Heart: This is a sacred space beyond the Sacred Heart (a sacred space above and beyond the heart chakra). It exists within the energetic system of the person's body. It is connected to the energetic and multidimensional system of their personal Higher Self beyond time and space. It is our personal Holy of Holies. Access to this Holy space can come only by way of permission from the Higher Self upon being deemed worthy to enter in humility and devotion.

Initiations: These are markers and ceremonies of progress. The lower initiations (the first to the fifth initiation) are based on light and karma paid. The Higher initiations (fifth to the ninth initiation) are based on the Ascension progress of the Higher Self.

Karma: Karma is the negative thoughts, words, and actions we have created in our past lives and in this life. All karma, past and present, is stored in our chakras.

Life Master: The Ascended Master who walks with you to help you with your life lessons. Many people feel closest to their Life Master.

Light Language: At the Ascended Masters' portal, we feel that "speaking in tongues" and "light language" are basically the same thing. For some, it may be channeled; but we have observed that this phenomenon can also be an internal expression that comes from within, rather than being given or channeled from an external source. Having this ability does not indicate a high level of Ascension; we have seen many levels of Ascension speak in this way.

Perfect Path Technique: A meditation technique that can be used to determine if you are on your perfect divine path (the path of your higher purpose).

Protection Grid: A personal and unique energetic grid that has been constructed by a team of Ascended Masters in the energy of the Ascended Masters' portal; this grid protects you for your lifetime from energetic and psychic attacks from the dark side.

Rays: The rays are the manifestations of the attributes/aspects of God, individualized and focused within the universe and within every person. There are eight rays of incarnation, and when we incarnate into each life, we are born with five of these rays. These five rays help manifest the life and spiritual lessons we are here to learn and attain within each ray.

Ray Attributes and Colours:

- The first ray is blue, red, or silver. This is the Ray of God's Will over Personal Will. It has the attributes of personal power, balance, focus, personal strength, and personal will.
- The second ray is yellow. This is the Ray of Wisdom and Joy.
- The third ray is pink. This is the Ray of Unconditional Love, kindness, and compassion.

- The fourth ray is white. This is the Ray of Harmony through Conflict.
- The fifth ray is green or orange. This is the Ray of Healing, Knowledge, and Personal Truth.
- The sixth ray is purple, ruby, or gold. This is the Ray of the Goddess and of Devotion.
- The seventh ray is violet. This is the Ray of Transmutation and Change.
- The eighth ray is the Rainbow Ray, as it contains all of, or a majority of, the first seven rays.

Reincarnation/Cycle of Rebirth: The act of our soul being reborn, life after life. Reincarnation is to repeatedly go through the birth-life-death cycle. We reincarnate with the purpose of paying our karma. The cycle of reincarnation/rebirth ceases when all karma is paid and cleared from the chakras.

Sacred Heart: This is a sacred place behind and above the heart chakra. The Sacred Heart and the Holy Heart exist within the energetic system within the person's body. They are connected to the energetic and multidimensional system of their personal Higher Self beyond time and place.

Soul Seat: The soul seat is normally between the heart chakra and the throat chakra, under the collar bone, and is the home of the soul while it's in body. This is not to be confused with the soul star chakra, which is above the crown chakra. Usually, but not always, the soul seat is the same colour as the Ascension ray. The soul seat is also the storage center for all past lives while in the body.

Spiritual Path: There are many pathways to Ascension; some are based in religion. Those pathways that have no religious affiliation are loosely termed as "a spiritual path."

Torus Technique: A meditation and connection technique that allows one or more people (with or without Ascended Masters) to meditate and work safely together across all dimensions and planes in balanced vibrational harmony.

Violet Flame Oil: An oil created by St. Germain and Ra-Mun, with the Masters of the Violet Flame, Archangels, Angels, and Devas of the Violet Flame, within the Ascended Masters' portal. The Violet Flame oil is a powerful manifestation of the Violet Flame. It transmutes negative energy stored in the chakras and allows karma to come forward for payment in a gentler way, unhindered by personal negative energy. It greatly assists in Ascension.

Chapter One

Carol Anne Halstead

Finding the Flow

"Peace comes from within. Do not seek it without."

Buddha

I'm forever trying to figure things out in my head, despite what the heart speaks. I think that's the Gemini influence in my natal chart—it is my ascendant (I love the irony of the term, given the topic of the book). I was born under the astrological sign of Cancer, which endowed me with a sensitive, nurturing nature and a strong intuition. My moon is in Pisces, which represents the ocean and our vast consciousness. Both Cancer and Pisces are water signs. What I have learned is that I need to be "in the flow" in order to feel right.

For someone who likes rules, order, and structure, though, it can get interesting. I prefer to feel safe and secure. I used to like to predict the outcome before I started anything big—I'm not a risk taker. No wonder the crab that moves cautiously sideways is the symbol for astrological Cancer. This has created an ongoing conflict within me:

do I follow my intuition and hope to stay in the flow, or do I follow a plan I think is safe and predictable? At times, I would be unable to choose and would move into a state of inertia.

When this inner struggle surfaced, it was always fear that held me back. It was deep, immobilizing fear of ridicule, of being shamed or criticized, or of making a mistake or a wrong move. It wasn't this way with most decisions—for the most part, I was pretty confident about what I set out to do—but there were other times when I became really stuck, and I only discovered the source of this inner trap much later in life.

All things considered, I had a pretty decent family and life growing up. My mother was a balanced, patient woman who was also sweet, humble, kind, and loving. My dad could be tough and gruff, but we knew his soft spot; he loved us. I had four siblings close in age—it was fun to be able to have a spontaneous game of scrub softball with them, or to build roads on the nearby sandy hill with their dinky toys. I had three older brothers, but I was the first girl, and so I bore the brunt of my parents' worries about adolescence (my younger sister has thanked me for making it easier for her). Both sides of our extended families were large, and we enjoyed our connections.

Essentially then, there didn't seem to be any basis in this life for these irrational fears of criticism and failure that I experienced. I attributed them to my "oversensitivity," which often left me feeling out of balance emotionally. I sometimes heard "toughen up" or "you are too thin-skinned." My sensitivity mostly felt like a liability.

It caused me to pull in. I innately wanted to avoid exposure. Although I had friends, I tended to avoid those heart-to-heart connections that some girlfriends had. I could sometimes feel myself losing my sense of boundaries because my inner response to someone else's needs or requests seemed to come first. I needed time alone to restore. I needed to learn to set boundaries for self-preservation while still striving to be compassionate and responsive to those in need.

It wasn't until well into adulthood that I saw that my sensitivity could be a gift rather than a liability—a gift for interpreting my world.

If I were to get a do-over, I would take these realizations and change my way of relating in the past. In those moments and situations in which I found myself withdrawing or already stuck, I would find a way to express my truth with kindness and strength. I would understand how important it was for me to get back "into the flow". I have found that I feel more balanced and at peace when I can take an honest look at what's happening, and take action where necessary. My intuition is my radar, and I'm still learning to trust it. It's my superpower. It always guides me back to balance.

I knew intuitively that there must be something more to God and religion than the teachings from Catholicism that I was raised with, but I did love the Sunday morning activities of attending Mass followed by a big breakfast (often with our cousins). The celebrations around the taking of the sacraments like my First Communion and Confirmation were happy events. I grew up with statues and icons of Jesus and Mother Mary in our family home. My mother had a particular devotion to the Infant Jesus, who was often depicted in the arms of His Mother Mary.

My mother would say her nine-day novenas to the Infant Jesus at times when we were in great need of some extra help. There was so much trust in the power of her prayer to intervene in our lives. I loved witnessing the purity and simplicity of my mother's faith. Mine was much different. I believed in God but didn't feel that strong sense of devotion that my mother never questioned. I just felt there had to be something more to it than unquestioning faith. Although it felt warm and inviting to be part of our church community, I felt I was missing something important.

This feeling was deepened by two personal experiences of hospitalization that I had as a child: first at four years of age, and then again at the age of twelve. Both were for kidney infections, and the first was life threatening. I missed my first year of school while I was at home recuperating the first time, whereas the second hospitalization was less dramatic, and I recouped over the summer vacation. I was in grade eight at that time and was terrified of my teacher. I witnessed her humiliating and shaming young learners in front of the class. I'm pretty sure my illness had to do with what I had been taking in all year in that classroom. Later, when I studied the basics of Chinese Medicine, I learned that the kidney meridian was associated with the emotion of fear.

While this made perfect sense for my experience in eighth grade, I couldn't equate my earliest experience of illness to this at first. At age four, I was so young and had no memories of anything in my life that could have caused this dramatic physical illness. It was only much later, and through the lens of a shaman/psychologist, that I was able to discover the connection. All that fear had stemmed from some past lives in which I had had some pretty terrible things happen to me as a woman who was openly spiritual. Darker times. The fear I experienced then had carried forward to this lifetime to be cleared.

Through shamanic work on some of these past lives, I was cleared of this acute bring-me-to-my-knees fear that used to show up on occasion; this deep fear that caused me to withdraw or become immobilized.

That fear was different from the self-protective, intuitive knowing that I would experience at other times, which would prompt me to choose or avoid particular options or directions. It was this inner knowing that led me to decide to become a nurse at the age of twelve.

My father was disappointed by my career choice; he had suggested a field of study that, back then, was a non-traditional choice for women (Engineering). I was grateful to him for his belief in my potential, but it changed our relationship—I fell out of favour. This hurt, but I stayed firm in my decision. Fortunately, we reconciled before he passed away, which was less than two years after I graduated. It was crushingly painful to lose my dad. He was only fifty-six years old when he died.

As my nursing career expanded into teaching and contract work, I continued to work within the confines of the traditional medical model of health care. Then one day, I read an article about an energy healing technique that had been subject to scientific study. It was called Therapeutic Touch, and it opened up a new world to me. I was intrigued and wanted to know more. I learned the technique and began to practice on family and friends. My two-year-old daughter would observe me and practice on her dolls. (And as it turns out, she has a natural healing ability!)

But soon I became aware of a layer underneath this energy work that began to surface for me. I began to feel that I really needed to find something more centered in me before I practiced; that I needed to be in a more peaceful state before I gave a healing. I tried meditation to find that more peaceful and grounded place. This was new to me. Devotion to an external God or Master I could understand, but going within? What was there? I began to follow a couple in the U.S. who channeled very high beings and offered uplifting meditations. I loved how I felt during and after the meditations. I started to think about the possibility of enlightenment. I wondered if it was an end point, like a pinnacle of spiritual achievement. I imagined it to be a bliss state. I really had no idea and no answers.

I read *Autobiography of a Yogi* by Paramhansa Yogananda and learned about an Eastern-disciplined path to enlightenment with a guru. I read and attended lectures by some of the rising Western teachers. It all sounded good and even inspiring.

I also continued learning about different healing modalities. Learning took place at multiple levels: I was learning about ways to help others through energy work, and was simultaneously learning that this work was also about healing myself. And, most significantly, it was a spiritual journey for me.

During this beginning phase, though, I have to admit to being less discerning than I should have been; I was a bit gullible at first, and had to learn not to accept everything I heard or read just because it came from a so-called spiritual source. I thought there must be a destination and a clear path to enlightenment. I am goal oriented—it's just how I think. The wonderful concept of being in the moment was hard for me. There was no real clarity.

However, I was very fortunate to meet five other women who lived in the same area as me, who were also on active spiritual journeys. We have had some interesting study and travel experiences together. It was sometime in 2013 when one of our group mentioned that she had conducted an Internet search for information on the Ascended Masters. She had come across the concept of Ascension on the Ascended Masters website. There were teachings, products, services, and ongoing readings available that could measure our progress toward Ascension. There was a quantifiable way to clear karma.

At last—a spiritual path that I could relate to.

Curious as always, I had a reading done in April of 2013 and started following the recommendations supplied. Even after all the time and effort I had expended up to that point on spiritual seeking, I learned that I was only at the second initiation. It was disappointing news. I had expected that all of the prior work that I had done would have had a greater effect on karma clearing. So I began using the violet flame oil on my chakras. This was a slow and methodical process. When clearing karma, issues do arise. I needed to take my time with this phase. I also gradually introduced some of the other oils when I felt ready.

In June 2014, I still had not passed the third initiation. I reviewed the recommendations and decided to get a protection grid. It took me more than two years to pass the third and fourth initiations. This happened in July 2015. I was then invited to join a growing network of people on a Facebook page who had also passed the fourth initiation while using the products and services from the Ascended Masters website. Here was a new community of like-minded souls. I continued having healings and following the guidance given to me by Verna Maruata and Waireti.

I finally passed the fifth initiation in May 2016. It was marked by an unexpected event—I was stung by a bumblebee. Two of my friends each commented "This is an initiation!" and Verna verified this a few days later. I was so elated and at peace when I read that all-important email from Verna. This had been my dream; anything beyond this wasn't important. I had achieved my goal. My karma was paid. I did not have to return in human form to start this journey again. The Earth is a beautiful home—but the time here can be hard. Now I felt complete. I wasn't on a mission anymore.

But my Ascension continued anyway.

We are each assigned an Ascension Master who oversees our progress to the fifth initiation, when all karma has been repaid and our chakras are one hundred percent clear. We are also blessed to have a Life Master and a Master for each of our emotional, mental, and physical bodies. These Masters are available to help us do the work of clearing our karma and to help us with the challenges we can experience while doing so.

I had four Masters assist me on my journey to the fifth initiation. I discovered I was on the second Ray of Wisdom, Joy and Lightness of Being . Jesus, who is a second ray master, was my Ascension Master and Mother Mary was my Life Master. Pallas Athena was my mental body Master; she helped me with mental toughness. I really relied on her at times when I was out of balance.

Jesus was also present on my emotional body and Serapis Bay on my physical body. Serapis Bay intimidated me—he is on the fourth ray of Harmony through Conflict—and I wondered what was in store for me. Certainly the hives I experienced for ten months after the bee sting were an issue. As well, I had a back injury around the time that I started this work and have been healing ever since. The injury represented a major karmic payment, and also taught me about where I was looking for support. I learned I needed to be in alignment with my own inner happiness and to cultivate this source of support from the inside out. It isn't that life is free of problems and hardships just because you are committed to a spiritual path. Events, injuries, and illness happen to everyone—karma must be paid in order to leave the reincarnation cycle.

With Mary as my Life Master, though, I felt right at home. I went to a Catholic girl's high school called Immaculata. We had a devotion day dedicated to Mary on December 8th, her Feast Day. I have always felt very loved by Mary, and still do. It was really hard for me to have to actively release Jesus and Mary when I reached the fifth initiation. I grieved. But it was necessary, for I was stepping into the unknown world of having a Higher Self. My Higher Self was becoming my inner guru. It wasn't until I passed the sixth initiation that my Higher Self even began to connect to me through my Holy Heart. I slowly became aware of a sense of maleness and the colour green, and it dawned on me that I might now be on the fifth ray of Healing, Knowledge, and Personal Truth. Verna confirmed this.

My connection with my Higher Self continues to grow. He is fully embodied at this point, now that I have passed the seventh initiation.

He has recently connected with me in a much deeper way. I now experience Him as profoundly loving and steadfast. I'm still "watery" and need to be "in the flow" in order to feel and function well, but my new relationship with my Higher Self is helping me find my balance when life events or unhappy encounters throw me off.

What I have also recently discovered is that being "in the flow" means recognizing God has a significantly superior plan in mind for me than my ego could ever imagine. I used to co-create "my way" and now I've finally recognized that if I co-create the "High" way, the results will be infinitely better. It's taken me my whole life to trust that God's intentions for me are based on unfathomable Love. Just accepting this truth has caused my Higher Self to move in so much closer in my awareness.

Now as my Ascension journey continues, I look forward to being of service: working together with my friends in Calgary as well as the people I have met through the Ascended Masters Portal in New Zealand. For now, I'm happy just going with the flow.

April, 2019

Chapter Two

Elizabeth Tackenberg

A Stirring in My Heart

"Climb the Highest Mountain"

Maha Chohan

Ascension. When I first read that this could be achieved in today's world, I felt a stirring in my heart.

And then, the more I read, the more confused I became. Where did this fit into my life? Where was I in regard to my Ascension? Could this really be achieved by me, or was it just something mentioned in the Bible that could only be accomplished by God's select few?

In 2007, I felt guided to receive my first Akashic Record reading to help relieve this confusion. In response to my question about Ascension, the following analogy was presented to me in answer:

> *I was walking toward the horizon and the sun was about to come up over the horizon line. As I walked, I was offering a helping hand to others who were lying*

or sitting down and wanted to stand up. I did not stop, but I helped them as best I could while still continuing on my journey toward the sunrise.

The Masters and Teachers of the Akashic Records gave me the following interpretation of the scene: I was steadily moving toward my Ascension while giving a helping hand to others that I passed along the way. The sunrise on the horizon depicted the dawning of the New Age. The sun still below the horizon line, yet with its light already becoming visible, represented how the influence of the New Age was already beginning to be felt.

Ascension does not happen after only one lifetime—it takes many. In 2016, I had the opportunity to receive a past life reading from Verna Maruata and Waireti. I was amazed to hear that I had lived a total of 16,020 lives. They said this was an average number of lives for those who are now ascending. At some point, we reach the lifetime where Ascension becomes possible and we decide to go forward with it. I would like to share with you some of the experiences that helped to shape my own Ascension journey.

During my childhood, there was one unusual experience of a spiritual nature that stands out most in my memory, which occurred when I was fifteen years old. While my family and extended family were attending a funeral in the countryside (for one of my elderly relatives), my grandfather fell ill and my father quickly drove him to the hospital, which was quite some distance away. Later that fateful day, while my older brother was driving my cousins and me to our grandparents' house, I looked out of the car window at the sky, and I suddenly felt my grandfather saying "Goodbye" to each of us in the car, his four grandchildren. While experiencing this, I gained the inner knowledge that he had died and was moving on.

As I silently communed with him, my heart became filled with a deep sense of peace. His passing was now known to me and, most amazingly, I was completely at peace with it. I did not mention this experience to anyone else in the car, or to any of my elders when we arrived at the house. And about thirty minutes later, my grandmother arrived to the house crying heavily and informed everyone that my grandfather had passed. Although everyone around me started crying, my heart remained totally at peace and I did not cry. I found this to be most remarkable.

The next phase of my spiritual life began when I was in university. Throughout my childhood, I had always been encouraged to do well in school, with the expectation that I would pursue a college education. Being inspired by European architecture, I chose a five-year architecture program at Virginia Tech in the USA. The program was very demanding of my time and energy, and by my fourth year, I felt burnt out. Additionally, I felt an impatient stirring in my soul for answers to questions about life.

As a teenager, God had told me that I would find these answers in New York City in the future—at the time, that seemed very far away and practically impossible. However, by the tail end of college, I was given an auspicious opportunity to temporarily leave campus to do a student internship with a solid company in New York City. While there, I started doing yoga, became vegetarian, and enjoyed a variety of natural healing modalities. In my conversations with others about yoga and healing, my thirsty soul finally started to hear some of the answers it had been longingly waiting for.

This kindled a desire to go even deeper into my yoga practice. Therefore, before returning to Virginia Tech to complete my formal education, I took initiation with a yoga group for mantra meditation.

With great enthusiasm, I started my meditation practice. And about four months later, I had a full spontaneous Kundalini Awakening.

I experienced an explosive amount of energy releasing from the base of my spine which moved involuntarily up and down my spine seven times, each time going a little higher. When this internal mysterious force hit my third eye, all form disappeared; I perceived a moving river of Divine Intelligence, and when it hit my crown chakra, I heard a booming, masculine voice. It was a brief cosmic moment that ripped away my entire existing belief system. I had to create a new belief system from the ground up, incorporating this new experience. Not easy.

For starters, I decided to temporarily suspend my yoga practice in order to stabilize, physically, emotionally, mentally, and spiritually. And secondly, I needed to return to university in Virginia to graduate! A friend suggested that I would benefit from professional help. This was a good idea, and I proceeded to work with a New York City psychotherapist via telephone until I graduated. Afterwards, I continued working with him in his office for a number of years. This brought me even greater emotional stability, insight, and maturity.

After graduation, I moved back to New York City and was blessed with a wonderful entry-level job in my field of work. I loved New York—I loved everything about it. Having moved from the beautiful, tranquil countryside of Virginia to such a large, bustling, and noisy city was a big adjustment for me, but while in New York, I continued finding the answers to my soul-searching questions. Having now stabilized from my dramatic Kundalini experience, I was able to gently resume the hatha yoga and mantra meditation practice that I had enjoyed so much. This brought me even deeper into the teachings of yoga, and closer to the guru of the organization.

A few years later, at the invitation of a friend, I met another guru, Paramahamsa Hariharananda, who was speaking in New York City for a few weeks and teaching Kriya Yoga, the form of yoga written about in *Autobiography of a Yogi* by Paramahamsa Yogananda. As I had found this particular book on Kriya Yoga to be most profound (and had been deeply moved by the kind and loving face of its author), I was motivated to attend this talk and hear what this guru had to say.

Upon meeting him, Paramahamsa Hariharananda immediately encouraged me to take initiation from him and to practice Kriya Yoga, which I did the following summer when he returned to New York City in July of 1983. This set me on a new course, which brought me more emotional balance and increased awareness in all aspects of life. After practicing the Kriya Yoga meditation technique for one year, it was obvious to me that I was experiencing a more positive outlook on life, with better health in general. Encouraged by this visible and significant improvement, I continued practicing daily for several decades.

In October 1985, I had the opportunity to travel with my guru to Paris for two weeks while he did a program there. Little did I know that I would meet my future husband on this trip, who was visiting from Holland and also attending the same Kriya Yoga program. Two years later when he came to New York to marry me, he gave me a choice regarding the country in which I wanted to live. I chose America. Then, to be fair, he got to choose where we would live in America. He chose Florida.

After a few years, we started a business together that capitalized on his various unique abilities. Over time and with a great deal of effort and hard work, the company became successful and well known within its industry. Once the business was up and running, I returned to my own professional work specializing in interior architecture, while still continuing to help him in our new business on the weekends and evenings. Then, once the business was finally running smoothly and had several employees, I was able to step back.

A STIRRING IN MY HEART

In 1996, Paramahamsa Hariharananda made both my husband and me Yogacharyas. He requested for us to initiate and to teach Kriya Yoga on his behalf. To be a Yogacharya is something very special, and it is not given easily or lightly. Initially I thanked my guru for the blessing, to which he replied "It is not a blessing. It is an opportunity." He went on to explain why this was, and as I experienced it for myself in the years to come, it became clear that it was, indeed, a responsibility that carries within it the opportunity to serve others.

I slipped easily into this role and did well. After a short time, though, my husband decided to stop and to focus on his work instead. I continued actively serving in this capacity, in my free time and on a voluntary basis (until my health forced me to gradually step back after fifteen years of dedicated service). During my tenure, I did local programs, retreats, initiations, and classes, and I also travelled to perform these services throughout the rest of Florida and the USA. I helped my guru establish an ashram in South Florida and I helped with the conceptual design and development of a new meditation hall.

The organization continued to grow. For many years I served on the Board of Directors, helping to guide and direct the ever-expanding and developing organization. It was an honour and a privilege to work with Paramahamsa Hariharananda—and later, his successor, Paramahamsa Prajnanananda—to spread the message of Kriya Yoga throughout America and around the world.

My first introduction to Ascension and the seven rays occurred in late 2006, when I picked up the booklet *How to Work with Angels*, published by The Summit Lighthouse. I immediately put to use several of the methods suggested in the booklet, and I experienced positive results right away. I continued this steadily on a daily basis for several months. About six months later, and just after my initial Akashic Records reading, I found The Summit Lighthouse's website and started reading through the material. Upon discovering their bookstore, I ordered a number of books and started reading more material about Ascension, and a whole new world opened up for me.

Soon I learned about St. Germain's Violet Flame decrees. When I first started saying them, I felt such an extreme burning sensation around my feet and ankles that I could only say the decrees for a couple of minutes. I learned about Archangel Michael's protection and how important it is (unfortunately, after a severe attack from the dark side). I learned about the Ascended Masters and their spiritual retreats in the etheric realm over our physical planet, and how to go there at night while sleeping to study with various Ascended Masters and/or Archangels. In order to access even more information on the website and to participate in online activities, I joined their fraternity. During this time, I learned a great deal about the Seven Rays, the Ascended Masters, and myself.

In 2007, I was introduced by a friend to Lily and Beyond, a protected energy system that was created by the Divine Source, which was still, at that time, in its early developmental stages. My association with this group advanced me in ways beyond explanation. By God's grace and with the blessings of the Ascended Masters, I experienced great leaps in expanded consciousness with an ever-increasing awareness into the higher realms of light, while at the same time remaining fully grounded in this reality. Having seen and experienced these higher realms, I no longer held any doubts regarding the continuation of life beyond this physical world. In addition, during my association with this group, I received attunements for a variety of energy healing modalities, and I learned how to read the Akashic Records proficiently. Occasionally, I would rent a room in town and give workshops and talks to introduce people to what I was learning and experiencing. I was encouraged to share my knowledge; I held healing circles and meetings in my home.

However, just as Ascension was coming clearly and fully into my world in 2007, my twenty-year marriage had started to unravel, and then came to full closure a few years later. I found this to be far more painful than I could have ever imagined. We suddenly found ourselves at a crossroads, and we were forced to choose. The path that my husband decided to take and the path that I decided to take were no longer compatible at a higher level of being, and God separated us just as mysteriously as He had brought us together.

In October 2014, I heard a conversation between two friends, one of whom had the ability to see auras. That person said to the other, "Why are you so pure? What are you doing to be so pure?"

The other answered, "I have found a website that has Ascended Master oils, and I use them. One of these oils is the Violet Flame by St Germain. I believe that this must be the reason you are seeing such purity."

That was enough for me. I requested the website information—www.alphaimaging.co.nz—and immediately ordered a bottle of oil infused with St Germain's Violet Flame. Additionally, I discovered that I could sign up for free weekly healing sessions by the Ascended Masters. I applied the Violet Flame oil as instructed and received a series of free healings from the Ascended Masters, both of which gave benefit.

In April 2015, I received a chakra reading report from Verna Maruata and Waireti. Based on this information, they were able to tell me exactly where I was in the Ascension process: I was getting close to the fourth initiation. With great joy and over a period of time, I purchased all of the long-distance healings offered on their website. I especially recall the past life healing because I could actually feel the Ascended Masters healing multiple old sword and bullet wounds.

This was confirmed by Verna in a follow-up email, shortly after the healing session was over.

I was amazed at how much healing had been accomplished in so little time and with no effort on my part, other than to purchase the healings. This was extreme grace.

Finally clearing one hundred percent of my karma from each chakra, I received an email from Verna on February 21, 2017, telling me that I had passed the fifth initiation and had left the cycle of rebirth. When I completed this initiation, I felt as if a great weight had been lifted from my shoulders. Life changed. I found that obligations were no longer searching me out; instead, opportunities were coming to me, and I had the option of choosing to participate in them or not. How delightful!

On April 10, 2017, I completed the sixth initiation, and my Higher Self was ready to begin his descent into my physical body. The descent of the Higher Self into the physical is a process that takes time because there is a lot of shifting, clearing, healing, and adjusting that needs to take place; also, it is a time for the Higher Self and for the Lower Self to learn how to work together. Early in this process, I felt inspired to go visit my family, as well as the places where I had lived during my childhood and the university where I had studied architecture. It was a beautiful trip, and I felt that my Higher Self was very happy to meet my family and to experience these places. While visiting these locations, I found myself resolving various long-held negative thought patterns and feelings. Consequently, as these issues melted away into nothingness, I felt an even greater respect surface for my childhood, schooling, and family.

It has been almost two years since this phase started, and I feel more balanced and stronger in many ways. My Higher Self is two-thirds of the way through this process, and I have cherished being home alone and being quiet during most of this time. My mind and body have required a lot of rest.

My Higher Self is of the Rainbow Ray, or the Eighth Ray, which is the first of the hidden rays. The eighth ray will influence my personality and life going forward. This ray combines all of the colours of the first seven rays into one ray. It is a ray of Unity and Integration. The Lords of the Akashic Records have told me that "this is a demanding ray, demanding excellence while contributing much to humanity." I will learn more about it over time, as I experience it.

Prior to passing the sixth initiation, the rays influencing my life and personality were different. It can be interesting to reflect back and to see their influence. The Five Ray reading that I received from Verna Maruata and Waireti back in 2016 revealed the following:

Rays 3-2-1-4-5:

- *3rd Ray—Ascension Ray, the pink ray of Unconditional Love with Mary Magdalene*
- *2nd Ray—Life Ray, the yellow ray of Wisdom, Joy, and Lightness of Being with Jesus*
- *1st Ray—Mental Body Ray, the blue ray of God's Will and Power with St John the Baptist*
- *4th Ray—Emotional Body Ray, the white ray of Harmony through Conflict with Serapis Bey.*
- *5th Ray—Physical Body Ray, the green and orange ray of Healing, Knowledge, and Truth with Hilarion*

St John the Baptist, serving on the blue ray, is known as an Ascended Master of meditation. We can easily see his influence on my mental body by my decades of meditating. Many times, especially when I was in my twenties and thirties, I felt that my meditation practice was my saving grace, because without it, I doubt if I would have been able to handle the stress in my life.

When I would guide meditation and yoga classes, the people participating would tell me that I had a lot of heart. I suppose that this was the influence of the pink ray with Mary Magdalene.

When I would give a lecture on Kriya Yoga or some related topic to yoga students, I often made the class laugh. My guess would be that this was the influence of Jesus on the yellow ray, bringing lightheartedness and knowledge.

Serapis Bey, serving on the white ray, is known as a very demanding Ascended Master. We can see his influence on my emotional body by the fact that I often needed to work with a therapist to help me sort out my feelings and to help me find harmonious ways to resolve the conflicts in my life. Since I have been on the Rainbow Ray, I have noticed a softening in my relationships. I hope this trend continues.

I chose architecture as a profession because I wanted to design buildings and to create beautiful three-dimensional living and working spaces. It is very physical in nature, and often friends outside of my profession would comment on how nice it must be to see my work manifested in the physical world at the completion of a project. It was true. I enjoyed that part of my profession very much. I suppose that this derived from a combination of rays: the pink ray, the desire for more beauty in the world; the white ray, creating harmony in the world of form; and the green ray, influencing how I saw the world and moved in it. After I stopped working in the field of architecture, I started doing energy healing work combined with life coaching for a few years. This reflected a combination of the green ray and the pink ray.

My journey toward Ascension has not only been an outward journey, but it has also been an inward journey, of moving out of my head and into my heart. Two chakra readings in particular confirmed this shift. My first chakra reading from Verna Maruata and Waireti, given on April 2015, indicated that my heart chakra was half pink and half green. They said that green was normal and that this change indicated that "your heart chakra is moving into a state of compassion and hopefully by the fifth initiation is completely pink." An updated reading given on July 2016 indicated that my heart chakra had become "completely pink;" I was told that "your heart chakra is coming more into a state of compassion and unconditional love." I attained the fifth initiation seven months later.

During this new phase of evolution, I found that, inwardly, whenever I would meditate deeply, my focus would be drawn into my heart due to a beautiful heat that started to stir there. Gradually, I discovered that the deeper I went into my heart, the more my heart would radiate blissful waves of love. Divine Love was dancing within my heart. The heat, generated by an intense light coalescing deep within my heart, sent streams of light out through my hands and feet and into the world. It was an exquisite meditation that I would sometimes enjoy for hours. I felt this meditation was very purifying and healing for me, for others, and for various parts of the world in conflict. Surely this advancement was strongly influenced by Mary Magdalene, my Ascension Ray Ascended Master serving on the pink ray, along with Jesus, my Life Ray Ascended Master serving on the yellow ray.

Also during this time of inner shifting from head-to-heart, I found that, outwardly, I had lost interest in architecture and wanted to work with people instead of abstract drawings and construction. So I obtained a certificate in life coaching. A local New Age bookstore hired me to do spiritual life coaching workshops. In these workshops, I would often guide the participants in meditations going deep into their hearts. Additionally, we would often talk about gratitude and compassion, and how to bring these virtues into everyday life.

Nowadays, I am getting to know my Higher Self. It started last year, a few months after passing the sixth initiation. While sitting quietly and relaxing one day, I suddenly became aware of a very kind, smiling face in my inner conscious awareness, looking down at me from somewhere just above my right ear. Who was that? After this happened a few more times, I had the idea that it might be my Higher Self trying to introduce himself to me. Yes, that was exactly what was occurring.

My Higher Self continues to reveal more of himself to me. I have found him to be extremely kind, friendly, outgoing, and good natured. He has blonde hair, blue eyes, and a young, vibrant body. Twice while attending church services, I saw him with enormous angelic wings. And once, while the priest was offering a prayer, I asked my Higher Self "What are you doing?" and he answered, "Praying." On a few occasions, I have felt him comfort me with his wings. I have been graced with a small glimpse of his great vastness, which has given me a hint of his world. I have even been blessed to hear his deep masculine voice a few times.

The stirring that I once felt in my heart when I first heard that Ascension could be achieved in today's world has been satisfied. My Higher Self recently told me that "we will serve the Rainbow Ray together; just follow my lead and you will enjoy every moment."

With such a beautiful promise, I am looking forward to our next adventure, together, in service.

February, 2019

Note: In August, 2019, Elizabeth passed the seventh initiation.

Chapter Three

Kathryn Murray

Inner Reflections:
Paths to Ascension

*"To everything there is season,
and a time to every purpose
under heaven."*

*Ecclesiastes 3:1
King James Bible*

Reflecting back on my life, I began with a sheltered upbringing in a small town in New Zealand. I recall the pristine rivers and our childhood swimming and picnic expeditions. As my life path moved forward, it led me to teeming cities, vast deserts, pyramids, and camel riding.

From a young age, I was aware of my parents' feelings. I sensed they were doing their best. I also understood I was to make a difference in their lives—through my presence, they experienced so much.

But my voice often landed me in trouble—talking in class and being punished, answering my father back and again being punished. This had a huge impact throughout my life. Statements like "be seen and not heard" and "stop asking such stupid questions" dampened my spirit. Behind closed doors, I voiced my frustrations. I sang, played guitar, and sang some more. I read books aloud for just the cat and myself. In high school, the patriarchal teachers had a knack for dampening my spirit of innocence and trust. So I created a protective barrier to avoid ridicule and criticism. This took the form of a feeling of low self-worth.

This feeling accompanied me as I moved on to nurse training. I struggled my way through. Once training was completed, I chose to leave nursing. The system did not sit well with me; I began searching in earnest. *Who am I? What is Life all about?*

Needing a fresh start, I headed south to Christchurch. Here I completed midwifery training. The experience I gained set me up for everything that followed. I experienced the raw emotions of mothers giving birth, the joys and grief. I shared tears with many. I discovered the unity underlying all human beings. I perceived a touching vulnerability and unconditional love, free of judgements. This is, for me, the essence of Being. I gave myself permission to surrender to a Higher Power. I explored meditation and yoga, practicing daily. This became a way of life. It was my spiritual hygiene.

My first marriage prompted me to explore my self-worth issues. I struggled with my feelings, especially the ones that left me disempowered to speak my truth. I was living a life that was not true for me. And so I made the decision to leave the marriage, and I began travelling overseas. Freedom was exhilarating; so much so, I continued for two years. I faced my fears all along the way. I learned to ask strangers for help. This was tremendously self-empowering.

Eventually my path led me back to New Zealand. Once again I was back in the family home. But I found I could not settle. Everything seemed so quiet. I felt that I didn't belong there anymore. I was floating. I was adrift. Resuming my travels, I let myself flow, following my innermost thoughts and feelings. I moved between countries on a whim. This time I took three years.

Then my parents heard of a natural disaster that had occurred in my vicinity. I was unaware of and unaffected by this, but nonetheless, they were terribly worried. This was in the days before the Internet; occasional telephone calls were the only method of communication. I heard clearly "It's time to return to New Zealand." When I arrived back at the family home, my parents were overjoyed.

But joy soon turned to shock with the sudden death of my mother. The grief was so raw. The devastation of her loss cracked me wide open. Again I felt utterly adrift. I discovered how my father grieved, and how similar we actually were underneath our daily masks.

I remained home for three months, healing, restoring, and nourishing my soul. And then, out of the blue, a job opportunity arose in Auckland. I grabbed it with open arms. I became an Air New Zealand flight attendant. Wow! How could this be? My workplace was like a dream. I was travelling the world and being well paid. I loved our passengers. Life became a stage. I was the lead actress. I met so many interesting people. I served them from the heart.

I married for a second time, enjoying an easy life and blessedly giving birth to a delightful daughter. As the years went by, I began exploring spiritual life by entering a church, wanting my daughter to have a Christian upbringing.

The church was vibrant. I loved the music the most, and it became quite mesmerizing at times. On one occasion, the notes and sounds of the repetitive music stirred something within me and I experienced a joy like never before. This stirring remained with me as a constant reminder of our God within.

However, after ten years in my marriage, I came to know that I was not on the right path. After much soul-searching and angst, and with a child to care for, I left a marriage for the second time.

And then my spiritual exploits began, in earnest. The Internet had arrived, opening up a whole new world. I began to meet like-minded people. I took a part-time nursing position in wellness. I had already trained in Reiki, and I learned massage as well. I was able to practice this service from my home and also at my place of work. I met Light workers who spoke in Light Language. I took courses and did retreats in self-development and spirituality.

Then I met Verna Maruata, an energy artist/healer (and much more). She was bringing the energies of the Ascended Masters through her paintings. Her knowledge of Ascension began with the building of an Ascended Masters portal. Verna sat with the energy of each Master, Archangel, Elohim, and Deva who have stepped forward to assist humanity, and painted their unique energy onto canvas. She was then given the gift of chakra and Ascension ray oils, healing shawls and a wide variety of tools to aid our Ascension. I now had valuable information and tools to assist my journey from the fourth initiation through to the seventh initiation, and counting. My path was clear. There was no stopping now. I began rising above dense old patterns. I was becoming aware of the inner Goddess warrior; I am She. *Who, me?* Yes, absolutely.

I journeyed from the fourth initiation to the seventh initiation with a soul family who had all been drawn to the Ascended Masters website at one point, in search of Ascension information. We had become friends through a Facebook group that had been set up for those who had passed the fourth initiation, and it has been wonderful to be able share our thoughts and ask questions along the way.

Once at the fourth initiation, we shared a common goal of passing our fifth initiation to free us from the karmic cycle of rebirth. This was a big deal. During this time, my Ascension teacher was the Ascended Master Quan Yin of the third ray of Unconditional Love. My heart expanded and softened into a much deeper understanding and knowing of love and compassion. This love is beyond romantic love. It is the love of All There Is. This was naturally steering me into finding more self-love, which had been lacking for far too many lives. My team of masters during this stage were from the second, third, sixth, and seventh rays, and they kept my focus upon my goal.

Even still, though, the path along the fourth initiation was a tough one for me in many ways, especially within my personal relationship with my new partner. He saw me go through periods requiring solitude, which were hard for him to fathom and he often felt excluded. I was often rendered unwell with headaches and sore throats, flu-like symptoms, extreme tiredness, and even severe dehydration. Twice I required intravenous infusion to rehydrate (I always drank large amounts of water, yet it was still not sufficient). It took a long time to realize that my body required more electrolytes and glucose during this time; the faster light frequencies had quite the effect on my cells, and for the first time in my life, I experienced hypoglycemia, low blood sugar. And so I learned to manage this by carrying glucose sweets with me, and then my symptoms quickly disappeared.

Otherwise, aside from cutting back on wine, my dietary requirements didn't change. This period seemed like such a long grind at the time, yet on reflection, I did okay. No—I did better than okay. I observed my self-judgements and became kinder to myself. Each ailment took me to a quiet place to ponder, to rest, to relax, to release stored anger, and this allowed for new growth.

Finally, after what felt like the longest time, my chakras one through seven reached one hundred percent light. They had been perfected, and all karma had been paid. I was ecstatic when I passed the fifth initiation. The moment wasn't marked by any bells or whistles, but there was certainly a sense of knowing that a shift had occurred.

Comparatively, my progression from the fifth to the sixth initiation took far less time, around three months. My Dimensional Lives Master was Pallas Athena, who showed me a strong divine feminine warrior aspect of myself that I'd never seen before. Although I do not actually see clairvoyantly, I have a sense of knowing (claircognizant) and feel empathically. And once I'd made it to the sixth initiation, I fixed my sights upon the next goal, the seventh. There was no turning back. My Higher Self was to descend into my heart, my body. A merger. Wow.

This merger took two years, and once again I was so grateful for the guidance and shared experiences of my fellow voyagers in our Ascended Masters group. I wasn't crazy after all! This was a period of many changes, which were mostly subtle, but when added up, they were life changing.

However, in the first few months following the sixth initiation, I remember feeling quite alone; my previous Ascension team of masters had stepped aside to allow for my Higher Self guidance to come forth. My ego was still active and alive; passing the sixth initiation hadn't miraculously vanquished old thought patterns. In came the thoughts of doubt: *Was I capable of hearing my Higher Self—or capable of anything?* With claircognizance (knowing) being my strongest gift, along with empathic feelings, I played the game of trying to discover which ray I was currently on. But nothing had sprung to my mind, and I was experiencing some self-doubt. And so I was guided to sit with each ray in turn, one through seven, to see if any of them resonated.

After spending a day with each ray, I realized how comfortable I felt within each of them. Feeling blended within each ray, a loud thought suddenly occurred to me: *Could I be on the eighth ray?* Once this thought arose, it became my next cause for self-doubt. At this time, no one else in the group was on the eighth ray, and there wasn't a lot of information about it. However, each time I tried to return to each ray, I kept getting: *You are on the eighth ray.*

Then I was given a brief flash of my Higher Self, and a resonating *Yes!* As soon as I accepted this as truth, I was also given that my own Higher Self was a slender and rather regal female with gorgeous, long dark hair and wearing a long ruby-coloured gown. She held a scepter, which had a large crystal or gemstone on the top. She was calm and gentle, yet held an empowered stance, quite the opposite of my own lower self. I felt rather emotional that she had chosen this physical vessel to occupy, and that a higher purpose of service would begin after the seventh initiation.

My Higher Self has her own Ascended Master teacher. This is White Tara, an eighth ray cosmic master. Reflecting back to when I first moved from the city to a small, rural, coastal village, we bought a home on Tara Road. We also had a yacht renamed *San Tara*. There are no coincidences. As I progressed through the sixth initiation, numerous physical ailments hit me once more, ensuring that I rested and had the solitude I craved and needed. Ascension had taken over my life and it required my total focus.

I sought out as much information as possible, and was soon introduced to the world of telesummits. The first summit I listened to was called "You Wealth Revolution." This opened up a whole new world for me and led to many other summits. The information from the guest speakers was like nectar to my ears. I read various books about Archangels. I read books about the rays and Ascended Masters. Sometimes, the information conflicted with the Ascended Masters site, but by that time, I wasn't in judgement. I was gathering knowledge for myself, and I was able to discern what felt right for me.

When nearly ninety percent of my Higher Self was in physical body, masters began to arrive whom I had not worked with before. I could tell I was being groomed for the last stages of the sixth initiation, to allow for an easy transition into the seventh. I was given dates for when my Higher Self would be one hundred percent merged, and with close guidance from Verna Maruata and Waireti at the portal, these landmark dates arrived—along with my small wings of pearlescent white and a hint of pale rose pink. Even though I couldn't see them and had no idea what they really meant, I recall having a vivid ego thought: *Really? Just small white wings with a hint of pink?* I was disappointed! It's true. I lost myself in comparing my wings with the description of seventh initiates ahead of me. This reaction was somewhat petty and only fleeting. It was my ego still trying to stay intact, and making one last stand.

The seventh initiation began with a rather serene lull for two to three months, and I felt like I was in a protective bubble. At the same time, having achieved the goal of passing the seventh initiation, a question surfaced: *Now what?* I wasn't exactly chatting with my Higher Self, and in fact, everything was very quiet. But as I settled into this void, I began to enjoy the peace and calm. It was like being in a safe space, awaiting further guidance. I was a lady in waiting. It was also a brand new year, 2018.

But not long into the new year, the strangest event occurred, right out of left field. My partner of thirteen years—who had always stood by my side through thick and thin, even though he thought I was gullible and easily led into strange ideas—had obviously felt neglected of my love and attention. He had a huge emotional outburst, said he couldn't go on like this and that he was leaving me. It was quite a moment. I felt a higher power fill my mind and heart, and I couldn't react. Instead I was held in a state of grace, cocooned in observation of the situation, quite devoid of all emotion. I heard myself say "NO, I WILL LEAVE!" followed by a brief moment of Lower Self thought: *gosh, did I really just say that?* It was so powerful and decisive. Time stood still, and I was only aware of a loud ringing in my ears, which I had come to know well—my Higher Self was in the house.

The outcome was beyond my Lower Self's expectations. My partner heard my words and asked me where I would go. Lower Self had no idea and couldn't respond. He did leave, for one night—and when he returned, we were both changed. It was time to restore our relationship, and we both spoke freely for the first time in years. I sensed my divine feminine merging within.

Over the following year, I was shown by my Higher Self (whose name had since been revealed to me during the sixth initiation: *Anaiyah*, Word of God) how to begin blending the divine feminine with the divine masculine. My path continued with the arrival of the next chakras of eight, nine, and ten. These chakras are all dinner plate size, and are placed where my base chakra, my heart chakra, and my crown chakra were formerly located.

There are many lessons yet to learn. I have become aware of some, and my partner has been a consistent teacher, reflecting my strengths and weaknesses. I acknowledge that I can only work on myself, and that a partner has his own journey. Yet as I change and grow, so too, does he. Our relationship is becoming stronger by the day, and our love is changing into something far deeper. My ego thoughts still arise and are quickly tamed by inner guidance to remain heart-centered, to breathe and think from the heart. On the Ascended Masters website, the Ascended Master Paul the Venetian provides a wonderful breathing technique that has since become my frequent go-to technique.

I am now a year and three months into the seventh initiation, with the next goal being the eight. It seems so very distant, but the full impact of working in service with Anaiyah is just beginning, and as I embrace the divine feminine and divine masculine within, a shift happens—to me, and all around me. One ripple creating waves.

My Ascension experiences have taken me deep within my physical body. They have become an energy tuning fork—I notice when there is a flat note. Receptivity for receiving and transmitting faster light frequencies from the Higher Self, Masters, and others from the beyond is clear. The emotional and mental bodies have undergone radical change as the ego is tamed, rested and educated to align with my Higher Self. Thoughts create words and symbols, which float across my inner screen. This process transmutes lower nature to higher nature, within Self and others. The brain balances in harmony, uniting imagination and will. This bond is light and playful. The inner child arises. The spiritual body renews with the power of love and compassion. How does this feel? Like walking simultaneously in two worlds. This has had its challenges. And yes, there have been headaches and fatigue. But there is always an urge to seek more. I am excited.

The interwoven threads of life's tapestry have always been there, dancing with the duality of light and dark. Shadows still arise. The old paradigm is now recognized. I have the tools to ease me through, clearing the way for a bright new world. I have retired from the workforce, and at sixty-six, I'm reinventing myself, accepting, at last, that true beauty comes from within.

February, 2019

Chapter Four

Elaine Marie

My Blue Flame Heart: Primal Love

"Now is the time for the full restoration of the sacred feminine template of the Christed Lightbody on planet earth. The embodiment of the living Goddess is achieved through our ascension into this Holy Body of Light"

Elaine Marie

Growing Up

I was born in the United States in a rural area of Maryland. We were what's known in America as a blue collar, lower middle-class family. We had a large extended family on my mother's side, and the family would come together for gatherings quite often. We always had a busy home and family life, and matters like education or psychological, emotional, and social well-being were paid little heed.

As the youngest of four children, I was always loved. They would say it was my ever-present smile and my innocent light. I was the favourite of grandparents, aunts, and uncles. I had a purity about me that attracted others. I spent much of my time playing in nature, and as I was too young to recognize the dysfunction occurring around me, I mostly remember a happy, carefree childhood. I realize now that I withdrew emotionally into my own imaginative world in order to instinctively protect myself from energies that I could not comprehend but that I knew were not good for me.

As I grew up, others began to recognize my "old soul" quality. I had a maturity that was uncanny to others, and could make them feel heard and seen at a deep level.

Throughout school, though, I did poorly and had little interest. I took to rebellion and partying in high school, and I finished with extremely low grades. But shortly after high school, I began to recognize that I was actually extremely smart, and very artistically creative. I simply had had no previous guidance as to how to direct or develop these gifts.

And with this realization, something finally clicked in me, and I was able to give up my self-sabotaging behaviours within a day. I focused on developing my intelligence, and even though I had very low grades, I set my sights on being the first person in my family to go to college. I spent one year in community college and, after receiving almost perfect grades, was then admitted to a four-year Catholic women's college.

While I had already rejected Catholic doctrine from my earlier, Catholic elementary school years, I was happily surprised to discover that the Catholic liberal arts college that I was now attending had nuns and women teachers that were powerful intellectuals; my mind was opened, as were my artistic gifts, as I explored literature, philosophy, political science, comparative religions, the arts, and all manner of thought systems. I felt I had found myself, and I became obsessed with the intellect; I read every book of classic knowledge and literature that I could get my hands on. My mind was insatiable for knowledge, and I was eager to reject the uneducated and difficult model of life that my family had presented to me.

I learned a lot about the cultivation of thinking in the world, and was fascinated by philosophies of morality and the nature and causes of good and evil. At this point, I was basically an atheist, or at best, an agnostic. I was disgusted by the false doctrines of religion and became an arrogant mentalist, discarding the mystical and esoteric as nonsense.

The Otherworld

Born as a Cancerian and an intuitive empath, I was highly sensitive to energies around me, both the energies of people and of the spirit kind. I knew spirits were around and could sense them deeply in my body. It terrified me and they knew it, so they seemed to enjoy tormenting me to keep me afraid as a child. I could sense them looking in the windows, lurking under the bed, doing all the things one does to scare little children. They were always behind me, chasing me up the basement stairs, giving me a fright. Sometimes when I went to old gravesites, a discarnate soul would contact me. Later I would figure out that they were not necessarily tormenting me, but were rather seeking me out to shamanically release them—but I didn't know this at the time, so when I felt their contact in my body, I became terrified and left immediately (I've since learned how to do psychopomp work to help newly deceased souls move from Earth to the afterlife).

It turned out that my whole family was very much attuned to this astral realm level interaction, although none of them had ever developed their gifts and sensitivities beyond the telling of their personal ghost stories. Everyone in the family had them. My grandmother had a great one: They had lived in an old, haunted farmhouse, with a civil war graveyard in the backyard. My grandmother was down on her knees one day washing the floor in a bathroom, when someone clearly pinched her on the rear end. Our family played a lot of pranks on each other, so she leapt up to find the culprit—instead, she found that there was absolutely no one else in the house with her.

Nature's Grace

Upon graduating from college, I decided to make a huge life change. My brother had already given up his steady job and had sold everything he had to live a new, carefree life in Colorado with his wife. So after finishing college, I followed him, driving two thousand miles from the East Coast to the Rocky Mountains in my beat up Ford LTD sedan with another friend, both of us looking for new adventure.

In the high mountains of Colorado, I was immersed in nature. Everything was about being outside, being active, being healthy. I challenged myself in amazing ways physically. I had amazing communion with nature. When I arrived in Colorado, I also noted the huge difference in the energy of the place. The dark, emotionally toxic environments of the East Coast, with its cities and unending suburbia, had taken a toll on me. I hadn't realized this, and wouldn't understand how significantly I had been affected by it until I discovered I was an intuitive empath and learned to handle this gift. I had been unconsciously eating dense dark energy from others my whole life. Colorado was a literal breath of fresh air. I avoided returning to the East as much as possible, except for a few brief visits to family here and there.

My Sexual Healing Journey

I had been sexually abused as a very small child. It created a conditioned reflex in my nervous system and body that left me frigid as a teenager and adult. My heart, mind, and body were completely disconnected from one another, and I had a paralyzing fear of intimacy.

Later, I also developed mental health and physical problems as a result of the intense resistance and anger that I had stored in my body, including severe depressions, chronic fatigue syndrome, and major metabolic and hormonal imbalances.

I was not able to sustain lasting adult relationships because intimacy recreated the experience of not being in control of my own sexual energy and personal boundaries. I had a deep and unconscious cellular belief that when I was intimate with a man, it would become a theft, and the only way to take control back was to play the role of seductress or to freeze myself into a state of numbness. And so I swung back and forth between these two patterns. Or, as another strategy of self-protection, I would unconsciously gain weight and effectively desexualize my body while in committed relationships, to repel my partner from me. At one point I put on forty pounds within three months.

Inside me thrashed a raging, rebellious, and terrified inner child who lashed out with entitlement and resentment for not being taken care of well enough, or because of men not being sufficiently dependable or reliable. I would shut down and become emotionally unavailable and vacant when anyone tried to get close to me. I had a deep sense of unworthiness in my body and could not believe I could be loved other than as an object of pleasure. I believed at a deep and unconscious level that if I lost my beauty, I would be rendered worthless and unlovable. This unhealthy and frustrating push-pull pattern destroyed my happiness and relationships, and left me deeply resentful, exhausted, and dissatisfied.

I have been on a long healing journey to unlock the mysteries that this wound has conjured up in my life and within my body. One of the most difficult parts is that I was so young when it happened. I do not have any memory of it. But the symptoms I've had all my life are textbook patterns of abuse victims, and I have had this truth confirmed by my Higher Self and by others whom I trust and who can see these things in our energy fields. I did deep spiritual work to clear victim patterns, anger, safety and boundary issues, but still found that the deep cellular memories and defense patterns remained. My body still retained the metaphysical scarring, even as my mind and heart began to heal and reconnect to one another. And so it was not until I added a physical aspect to my healing process, through a combination of tantric yoga, tantric breath and bodywork, and various somatic release techniques, that my body began to gradually open, disarm itself, and regain its vitality and expansion of pleasure states.

These puzzling clues took many decades to unravel, and ended up being core to my lessons and gifts as a healer in this lifetime.

Three Dog Nights

After a year or two of outdoor adventuring in Colorado, I began to grow restless mentally and decided that I needed to go back to graduate school. By this time, I had been dating a man for a few months, and after backpacking in Hawaii for a month, we moved ourselves to Bozeman, Montana. My plan was to work for a year to qualify for state tuition, and then apply to the university there.

Well, our life path has a way of diverting our course. It seems my partner and I had a soul contract to bring some beautiful souls into the world. My first son was born in Montana, where a really cold night is playfully called a "three dog night" because you would want to cuddle up with all three of your sled dogs in bed to keep warm. A few months after my son was born, we moved to Louisiana to be closer to my husband's family, to have more family support nearby.

Culture Shock and Calling

Louisiana was an absolute culture shock for me. Now a parent, my responsibility impulse kicked in and I began to make plans to begin a career in the nonprofit sector. I felt like I couldn't work in corporate environments (which I had experienced previously) and I deeply wanted to help others and to make a difference. I was soon hired in my new family's church food pantry as the part-time director. This began a sixteen-year career in a variety of nonprofit settings, working with homelessness, hunger, and social services. I learned a lot about the problems in the world and how things were affected by broken systems, public policies, and inequitable socio-economic structures. I became an advocate for the have-nots. I was really good at my job. I was a natural leader and, at a young age, took the helm of the organizations I was running and helped them grow. I became a local community leader and advocate for social change. I got a Master's degree in nonprofit administration. I had my second son, a job I loved, a lovely home, and family life.

My life was unfolding well enough. But underneath, something was stirring. I never really enjoyed living in the South. It was another unnatural place to me, energetically. So I decided to move my family back to Colorado, which I missed desperately. And I also admitted to myself that I had married my husband only because of our unplanned pregnancy, and knew the marriage needed to end. I felt dead deep inside.

Once I was back in Colorado, my work moved into environmental policy, and I ended up applying my administrative leadership skills to a job in a major university. I learned about climate change, public land issues, and renewable energy from some of the best scientists in the field. It was eye-opening, and as I possessed a skill set in the policy side of things, I became more involved in how to make changes through public policy and lobbying efforts. Through this experience, I was opened to the inner workings of power, and how things got done in the world—or didn't.

MY BLUE FLAME HEART: PRIMAL LOVE

Becoming Someone Important

Meanwhile, my home life had dissolved—I had asked my husband for a divorce and I became a workaholic single mother. These were tough years emotionally, as I put all my energy into my work, had a terrible and painful custody battle, and had little energy left for my kids and virtually none for a social life. Looking back, I can see I was acting like my own parents, who worked and supported the family's physical needs but were emotionally unavailable to their kids and others. I could only relate to others through the safe boundary of the professional work persona that I had created, and had difficulty with intimate friendships—especially with men. Whenever I'd attempt to have a relationship with a man, I'd quickly find myself becoming angry, disappointed, emotionally unstable, needy, unreasonably demanding, and controlling. My chronic fatigue syndrome worsened, and I struggled to maintain balance in my leadership positions as stress and pressure rose.

My emotional imbalances began to resurface in serious ways. I kept pushing myself towards higher level positions that would validate my ego and secret low self-esteem; I was lured by the prestige and power of politics. I even seriously considered running for some local political office, and began to learn more about this process. I was being fueled by a strange combination of motivations: truly wanting to make the world better through meaningful social change, and the desperate need to be seen as an important and respected person—the need to not feel invisible.

But no matter how hard I tried, there always seemed to be an intangible force that threw a shadow on the visibility I so urgently sought after. I was always in the invisible background. My talents and gifts were not acknowledged fully, and I was often brutally invalidated by the large personalities I was working around.

However, there were times when I did find the courage to make sure that I wouldn't be ignored—when I was forced to stand up to powerful people who abused their power. I never understood where this inner courage and strength came from, as I truly had no power in these crazy arenas, but this strength was called upon on more than a few occasions. Often I was protecting those who were under my care and guidance as staff, or standing up for others who did not have access to their own empowerment.

The End of My Career, and the Start of My Spiritual Path

My final formal leadership position ended with my resignation—what I had been hired to do was impossible, and I had to bluntly communicate as much to the Board of Directors. So I left my last role and moved into consulting.

And then, after a year of working as a nonprofit consultant, I ended my career. I remember that last day. I had my final client meeting, and then I walked out of the conference room very calmly and said goodbye. I knew that was it, but for some reason, I felt very calm. I no longer needed to bear all that responsibility for an entire organization. Indeed, I couldn't have handled all of that responsibility anymore, once the Ascension process had begun to "rearrange" my brain.

This is when, suddenly and a bit out of nowhere, my spiritual blueprint began to take on a major focus in my life. It was so sudden and life changing. Everything simply rearranged, and all my old life patterns and situations ended abruptly.

A few months after my career had ended, I was told to put everything in storage, sell my house, and make arrangements for my kids to go live full-time with their father and grandparents an hour away. I was heartbroken that my then eleven year old and sixteen year old would be leaving me. This heartbreak has never completely ceased on this entire journey—even now.

I have known some who have been able to hold down a job and keep their life the same during the Ascension process. But I know that I couldn't have. I felt like my mind was quite literally melting. In fact, it *did* melt. You have to melt down the control of the rational mind so that the higher mind can be developed and trained, and the heart-mind can take over. The rational mind is so limited. So yes, for a time, it felt as if my IQ had started to decline. I was happy if I didn't have more to think about than having to manage washing the dishes. When I tried to entertain the idea of a work project to earn some money, simply reading the job descriptions and seeing how task-heavy they were was enough to send me running away from the thought. I truly could not have handled such work. Not at that time. Not even *after* having mastered it, over many years. So formal work ended.

I went from being extremely mental and intellectual to being a bit of a simpleton—and it was terrific. I would crack up to myself when someone would start talking about worldly things or lofty intellectual ideas. I could care less. It was all based on faulty third-dimensional thinking anyway. While I used to be a voracious reader of knowledge, now I would only read spiritual books, and over time, even those had nothing in them that was interesting or new. So I stopped reading. There was nothing new to learn from a book. I liked it as my heart grew and my mind receded. I was so much happier. I was so much wiser as I learned to tap into and trust Universal Mind, which is infinite and all-knowing.

A Sadhvi

After my career ended, my spiritual guides told me that I was a sadhvi now. In Hindu, this is a female renunciate or holy person who leaves worldly affairs to pursue only their spiritual journey. It was so. I did not work again in the same way. My healer's work came and went as I progressed on my Ascension path, but very sporadically. I had a client or a workshop here and there, as I tried several times to launch my spiritual practice, but always something happened. It always dissolved. I always had to move or was getting thrown into a totally new and unfamiliar situation, which kept me from building any momentum. I became frustrated many times, especially after I'd become financially ruined about three years into the journey. I had to default on my debt, and was penniless for two years afterwards. I lived on the support and charity of my loved ones, and there was always a friend, family member, or loved one to step in. I had soul contracts to ensure that I would be cared for, but it was not easy.

I had to learn to be dependent on the kindness of others. I had to learn what it felt like not to have any choices other than the ones my Higher Self presented me with. I was essentially homeless but for the grace of whoever would give me a roof over my head. I had to surrender to my Higher Self totally. I went where she led me, and stayed where she provided for me, even leaving situations where I was very happy—leaving home; leaving my children to travel; leaving relationships with men whom I loved; letting go of possessions again and again. But always, I was taken care of. I was always in a beautiful place, but always faced with a need to surrender to what was happening, to not resist my lack of choice.

As a Cancer who is all about "home," this period of homeless was very challenging for me. But my Higher Self was teaching me that home is the earth, home is wherever you are. It is not a building or a place. You belong to the entire world.

At the end of this two year period, which is when I am writing this now, my clothes have become threadbare and I have very few possessions, and even less money.

The Body Transforms

As I approached my seventh initiation, my body began to transform. I was guided to learn tantra yoga, and after six months of daily practice, I lost the forty pounds that I had put on two years earlier, when my hormones went way out of balance as I manifested my de-sexualization strategy. During those two long years, I had no energy or stamina; I was in bed much of the time. So as I began the very long process of healing the sexual trauma, the weight began to melt off.

Every piece of clothing sagged on me, but I could not afford to buy new things. Underneath, as my body began to be reformed and made of light instead of carbon, I radiated health and vitality. I also had to ration my eating as funds tightened, which certainly helped the weight loss in tandem with the daily tantric yoga practice. I only ate twice a day, and very simply. I learned to live with very little, yet I always had so much. I guess this was part of my first ray warrior training.

I could see myself getting younger; my body was regenerating itself. Others noticed, too. They'd asked, "What are you doing? You look amazing!" Or they would say, "You keep looking younger every day," puzzled.

To those who understood, I would explain that it was the Ascension process; to others, I would credit the yoga and diet. So as I underwent this massive energetic recalibration, my energy began to return, my health returned, and my body felt amazing. I could feel my power and strength returning. I was reborn as a body, and then my seventh initiation began.

The Sounds of Creation

I always loved music. I would get chills and goosebumps every time I attended a concert or listened to soaring classical, choral, or opera pieces. I didn't know why that was at the time, but of course, it was the energy of sound resonating deeply in my body. Everything in creation sings. Sound, whether spoken or sung, is the primary vehicle for creation. Prayer is invocation of divine light, and singing our prayers adds a forceful momentum of emotion that animates life. It is very powerful. It is like an ongoing act of creation as devotional bliss.

Listen to nature. Everything is singing: the insects are a major symphony; the trees dance with the winds that blow in their leaves; the soft swooshing of the ocean; a cat purrs; the birds, the whales, the coyotes. In fact, some clever soul figured out how to slow down the sound of crickets and it sounds just like an angelic choir. It is the grand symphony of creation.

So my innate love of music carried over from my soul essence. I loved to sing, but only did it around the house. When I was living in Colorado in my thirties, I would spend my entire two-hour work commute singing different songs. It was the most fun I would have all day. This led to an interest in actual voice lessons, which I took from a professional opera singer named Alex. He exhibited tender patience as he took his beginner students through the rudiments. I couldn't read music, so that added another interesting challenge. I played music by ear, so I had to hear each song before I could figure out the sheet notes. I trained my voice and opened my vocal chords with tunes from popular musicals, classical pieces, and some beginner opera. Then, as my spiritual journey began to progress, I ended the lessons.

One weekend I was at a women's dance campout in the remote Rocky Mountains, and one of the exercises was to find a spot in nature that we were drawn to and to try to commune with spirit. I was drawn, as I usually was, to the aspen trees. As I sat quietly, Mother Mary, who is my life teacher, came to me and said one word with great emphasis. "SING!"

I didn't really understand this at all, as I had not yet made any connection between singing and spiritual things. I sang Ave Maria to the group of women. The group leader, a beautiful shamanic woman, said she saw Mother Mary standing next to me, just like in the Beatles song. It was powerful indeed, and the group was very moved. I still didn't totally get it, but it was then that I was led to the world of sound healing.

My vocal chords actually began to change. Over a period of a few months, they opened up so that my range increased significantly, and the range of sound and overtones, as well as the power of my vibrato, became quite increased. My singing teacher would have been delighted. He was always complaining how I constricted my throat, causing me to miss the higher soprano notes. My throat chakra had been very blocked at that time.

But now, my Higher Self was making alterations so that I could use sound to heal, I could actually feel this changing inside me. Once my throat chakra had totally opened, I couldn't believe what could come through me. And then one day, as I was making silly sounds in the bathtub to practice, a funny language started to come out. I somehow *knew* this language, better than I knew English. I didn't know how to translate the language directly, because unexplainably, it was not translatable into English. A whole series of sounds might represent an emotion or sentiment. It was a nonlinear language and it sounded like an ancient indigenous tongue. It was the language of light.

I also found my inner shaman, who is a very powerful healer, and many ancient chants and soul songs would come through quite naturally. Now I use it to channel high frequency light via sounding for healing. I still love to sing. Funny thing is, now whenever I sing a love song, I am singing it to my Higher Self with complete adoration. I have never been in love like this before.

Healing and Shamanic Remembering

One doesn't select the occupation of shaman—one *is* or *is not* this.

When this word first appeared in my life, I had a vague image of a dirt covered, hairy, crazy man chanting bizarre things and dancing oddly in the jungle, feeding insects to people. I had no interest in getting any closer to this word.

But all of a sudden, I kept getting tapped on the shoulder. Psychics I didn't know would tell me that I'm a shaman, or that I "need to follow the shaman's path" as I walked by them. It happened about three times in a short period of time, and so I decided to look into it a little bit more.

I went to a beginner shamanic training weekend. It was like I already knew everything; it was totally natural. I continued with another level of training and figured out the names for the healing work I had already been doing but had had no idea it was shamanic. I realized I knew much more than what was being taught in the schools, so I stopped going to the trainings. I already knew how to do this. There was an inner shaman in me that was very powerful.

My Five Year Journey to Ascension

I have been a part of two group Ascension processes, both sponsored by close contact with the Ascended Masters and Archangels. Each one was very different, yet they in no way contradicted each other.

I first came to the Ascended Masters portal in New Zealand, and have continued on as a close part of this Ascension group as I finish my seventh level of initiation. But I also spent five years in Jim Self's Mastering Alchemy program with the Ascended Masters and Archangels, training in advanced alchemy and activation of the Adam Kadmon Blueprint Light Body. I am grateful to have had both perspectives on this process, as each gave me a wider understanding of what is possible in this time of modern Ascension. They have tracked flawlessly next to one another.

Why would one take on the task of this Ascension process? What sparks the drive to make this final ascent up the mountain of human destiny and purpose? When I have asked others who have taken this journey, the most common answer I received was an indescribable knowing, or urge, or a feeling of coming home—a certainty. They just knew they had to take this journey, and often they can say little else about why or how they knew. It was like a homing device buried deep within them that had gone off. It just made sense in some strange fantastical way, when nothing else really did. I too have felt this way. I have known, without being able to actually explain how, that this is my purpose here.

I lost interest in worldly things while moving through this process. I changed everything about myself. Or, more accurately, these things just fell away. There were times when I have been so removed from the movements of the mainstream culture that I appeared a strange and detached fool of sorts to others who might venture an inquiry here and there about what I was up to in life. I did indeed become the divine fool. Where once I knew and followed the dramas of change, social unrest and injustice, and ordinary life on this planet, now I was mostly hidden, mostly alone, mostly spending an inordinate amount of time looking within, trusting blindly where I was being taken. People were shocked—some were horrified—and thought I was stupid or insane.

Ayahuasca

All spiritual traditions seem to have the same advice when people first begin seeking: *Look within*. What a surprise for me to even begin to unravel the multitude of levels of this *within* realm. I faced the daunting task of examining each shady morsel of the fear-based conditioned self and its motives and habits and blind spots, and journeyed towards the deep dissection of this self. I felt my God-self move within me, like the feeling we have when our prenatal child first flutters within our womb. I could feel her move energy throughout my entire body like a tidal wave. I actually met this God-self, in moments when she would appear as a vision and talk with me without saying a word. I adjusted to having this God-self live inside my own flesh, as a constant presence and a knowing and an explosion of love in my sacred heart.

We are complex beings, multilayered, multidimensional, so vast, so ineffably vast. I have not even scratched the surface in the exploration of what lives inside me. The entire cosmos and all of creation lives inside me. I could not possibly explore it all in any small human lifetime.

However, the vision I received towards the end of my sixth initiation was the most profound. I was told to go to an ayahuasca ceremony in Colombia. In these days of spiritual awakening, many people use this profound plant medicine in their journey to overcome the mind for a short time and be pushed directly into multidimensional reality, often in a terrifying way, to reach the astral realm. But for me, my journey was a journey directly to my God-self. I saw and experienced myself as Goddess, firsthand. In those moments, I just *knew* with so much veracity. I was certain who I was. It was laughable to be otherwise. She was fierce, with a Kali type energy, a warrior, a tantric master; and she kept saying in a loud voice YOU ARE THE DIVINE MOTHER! YOU ARE THE DIVINE MOTHER! It was a profound state of samadhi, which is defined by Paramahansa Yoganada as "perfect union of the individualized soul with infinite spirit" or "a state of oneness; complete absorption".

I also saw clearly that it is only when we can conceive of the complete dissolution of the little self that we can even begin to fathom the limitless nature and frequency of our God-self. Nothing can touch you after you have had this experience.

One of my favourite prayers helps to put this experience into context:

I am nothing.
God is all.
Therefore God is where I AM.
Therefore I AM that I AM.
Therefore I AM nothing.
Therefore God is where I AM.
Therefore, I AM God.

Auyasuasca is actually referred to as "the death vine." The ancients used it as an advanced initiation to complete the death and rebirth experience for the advanced shaman.

I will never be the same, and I am deeply grateful for this experience. And as St. Paul, now the Ascended Master Hilarion, also said, "I die a little more every day." It is an ongoing process. It never seems to end. As more of the false self slips away, more of the authentic divine self can express itself, without interference, as pure essence.

Now I am complete with the seventh initiation and I am fully a first ray, blue flame soul expression of my Higher Self. We came to be a living embodiment of feminine divinity.

I AM Fierce, Primal, Blue Flame Love.

February, 2019

Note: Elaine Marie passed the seventh initiation in March, 2019

Chapter Five

AmayahGrace

My Spiritual Journey...from four to seventy-four...(and counting!)

"This is the Book of Your Life - it's open...read it one page, one moment, at a time"

This is the story of my transition from a sad and lonely little four year old to a vibrant, joyful, passionate, and powerful woman in her seventies. As you read it, you will understand this introduction which Higher Self gave me.

I was born in the UK, and when I was about four years old, I had my first spiritual experience—I saw a fairy in the woods. She reached out and told me I had special work to do. I was so excited, I went running to tell my mother about it. Without looking up from the kitchen stove, she said "That's nice, dear. Now eat your lunch."

I was so deflated; I made a vow, there and then, to shut down that open, receptive part of me, and to retreat.

MY SPIRITUAL JOURNEY…FROM FOUR TO SEVENTY-FOUR…(AND COUNTING!)

Growing up, I always felt like I was the odd one out in the family: I was blonde and my two siblings were dark-haired; they were close in age (eighteen months between them) and I didn't arrive until seven years later. The age gap was too wide for me to join in their activities (not that they would have wanted a much younger sister to get in the way of whatever it was they were doing; I understand that now, but couldn't at the time). The feeling of not belonging was so persistent that I can clearly remember saying to my mother that I only had her and my father's word for it that I was their daughter.

Then, in my early teens, I discovered that there had been a still-born brother who would have been eighteen months older than me. Once I knew about him, I felt drawn and attached to him. I spent many years feeling as though there was part of me missing (after all, he would have filled the gap in my heart and in the abyss of years between me and my older siblings). Then a channel told me that we had been together in many lifetimes before, and that we had chosen to be apart in this life so as not to end up hating each other.

That feelings of not belonging followed me through my years of high school and secretarial college, which were largely characterized by struggles with low self-esteem, shyness, attempts to fit in, and periods of depression. I had been put off of the idea of going to university after conversing with chums who were already there—not one of them knew what they wanted to do when they graduated. The idea of spending all that time and energy with no end in mind seemed absolutely pointless to me; even if I had gone, I had no leaning towards one subject or another. I felt the professions were closed to me because my brother was an accountant and my sister a physiotherapist. At one stage, I toyed with the idea of doing law, but my disillusionment about going to university meant I certainly didn't want to do that. So my mother eventually decided where I was going for me: to London to do a two-year bilingual secretarial course. Bless her; she was absolutely determined that I wasn't going to fall into the traditional younger-daughter role of staying at home to look after her parents in their old age. I am grateful for her loving courage.

But old emotional patterns die hard—life in a London college and in the workforce wasn't easy for me, as I continued to struggle with my self-esteem and depression.

Then, in the mid-70s, my anchors—work, living arrangements, a relationship—all began disappearing. I remember hearing my inner voice say, *then I'll go travelling*. So I came to New Zealand, where my brother and sister-in-law had emigrated a few years earlier. There were so many synchronicities involved in the decision. When I look back now, I am in awe of it all. My original intention, or so I had thought, was to simply pass through, to travel around the world, and then to pick up where I left off again. But my true path was a very different one. I've only been back to the UK for the occasional visit since then.

I knew the instant I flew into Wellington, New Zealand, that this was *home*. It was like putting on a comfortable old overcoat that I'd forgotten I had; the place, the entire country, just wrapped itself around me. I wasn't able to put this feeling into words until some years later: at the end of a nostalgia visit to the UK in 1990, I knew where I belonged. I announced, "I'm now ready to go home," and then applied for New Zealand citizenship as soon as I got back.

My life of employment in New Zealand consisted of some years of office work, until I became a conference organizer for (what was then called) the New Zealand Society of Accountants. This was a gentle turning point for me; tasked with running presentation skills courses for the Society's presenters, I found that the act of teaching nurtured and inspired me, and it felt so natural to be standing up in front of a group.

In the years that followed, I focused on work and friendships, and started on a tentative exploration of spirituality. I read *Autobiography of a Yogi* by Parahamsa Yogananda (the starting point for many people's journeys) and Jane Roberts' *Seth* books, which I read and reread.

I discovered Julian of Norwich from reading a historical novel and felt so drawn to the idea of being an anchorite—echoes of more than one lifetime in religious orders, and not all of them joyous or uplifting. Her life and words resonated so strongly with me. I can remember being stuck in traffic one day, on the drive home from work, feeling depressed and hopeless; I heard my inner voice say, *all shall be well, all manner of things shall be well.* And then I burst into tears of relief and release, not caring who saw me in neighbouring cars.

Next I started meditating and doing reiki, and embarked on a series of self-development courses which, for a while, seemed to take over my life. They allowed me to start understanding my own background and patterning, and to begin the life-affirming work of releasing and freeing myself of those patterns—it's a process that is ongoing.

I also developed a fascination for, and an understanding of, how our experiences impact our lives; this is now at the core of my client work.

What I learned and experienced during this self-development work changed the course of my entire life. For starters, I began meeting new people. Every Sunday, a group of us would get together for meditation, chanting, yoga (yoga wasn't my scene—I'd take myself off walking over the fields and in the bush instead; how I loved that time on my own) and then lunch. These were magical days.

Big things happened during this time. The first was in the beginning of 2000, during one of our Sunday lunches; somebody talked about a guided trip/pilgrimage she'd done in Peru, and I instantly *knew* I had to do it—and do it that year.

In preparation for the journey, I was told to write my will. I resisted doing this for many months because I knew I was safe and that nothing untoward would happen to me. Looking back a couple of years later, I realized that the old "me" *had* died in Peru—my life and my focus started to change after that.

Peru was a real turning point for me. I had a magical, mystical experience at Sillustani, where we had been told that we would receive a gift, "something you've been yearning for." I had no conscious knowledge of what that could be, but I found myself weeping once we'd arrived, and had leaky eyes for the rest of the day. Later in life—when I discovered that I had the ability to heal people by touch—did I come to understand that at Sillustani, I had had my healing abilities restored.

The first demonstration of this was on a Sunday shortly after I had returned to New Zealand. I was standing in a circle with the others when the lass next to me kept moving and flexing, as if she was trying to get comfortable. I saw my hand go out to the small of her back and vibrate slightly. She looked at me as if to say *What on earth?* and I just looked back and shrugged my shoulders—I had no idea what was happening.

After about a minute, my hand came back. She quietly said, "Thank you."

"You're welcome," I replied, with absolutely no idea of what had just occurred.

This same person came up to me a few weeks later and said "You weren't to know, but I had had a bad back for about four years, and now it's gone. It went shortly after you put your hand on it."

A few Sundays later, the woman who hosted these gatherings was unusually quiet and pale. As people were leaving in the afternoon,

I gently asked if she was okay. She said she'd been experiencing the start of a huge migraine. I heard myself say "Would you like me to give your head a massage?" without any idea of what to do. I panicked when she happily accepted. I sat down on the sofa and she sat on the floor between my knees; as we got settled, I watched my hands position themselves on her head, and then very gently massaged her there with my fingers. After a minute or two, I watched my hands move to a different position, so I started to massage there. This happened once more and then, suddenly, I knew she was done. When I rang her the next day, she told me that what I had done had reduced a four-day migraine to a day and a half.

After that, I massaged people's heads and shoulders and backs, all the while knowing that there was a healing component to the massage. I gradually started doing full-body massages, completely untaught, using movements that my body remembered receiving and enjoying, and others that just seemed to flow from the process and that clients loved. They reported experiencing healing as I massaged them.

After Peru, there were some years of exploring various modalities to add to the healing massage. I felt the need to have a professional title as a practitioner of some recognised form of healing or therapy, all in an effort to validate my skills and, by extension, me, so that I could stop feeling like a fraud. It took me many years to acknowledge that I channelled healing energy, and even longer to see that, in truth, I *am* a healing channel. It is who *I AM*, not just what I do.

Another second important thing that happened shortly after I returned from Peru was on one of those lovely Sundays on which I left the others to their yoga to go for a walk. I was wandering over a steep paddock along a sheep track when I turned my ankle very badly. I knew I was too far away for anyone to hear me calling for help. I must have been divinely guided because I heard my voice say to my ankle, very firmly and very clearly, "Heal!" And I could feel all the cells in the tendons and ligaments return to their normal size and place. Then I simply walked back to the house—no limp, no soreness, no swelling, no bruising. I recognize now that I was being shown the power that our thoughts can have over our bodies, for health and for disease, and this now informs much of my client work.

Also around this time, I went on a Wesak retreat in Australia to celebrate the spiritual birthday of Buddha. During that weekend, I sent up a request: *If you want to use me, please let it be for something important.* I had no idea what I was asking for—it certainly wasn't ego-motivated, and the wording didn't feel like it was mine—nor did I know whether my request had been heard. Now, I do.

The following year, I did another Wesak retreat, this time just north of Wellington. On one of the last meditations of the weekend, I was shown a book with my photograph on the cover, but the name on it wasn't mine; it started with an *A*. I had no idea what all that was about, but was to find out shortly.

The next turning point in my life was at a retreat where I met Verna Maruata. A few months later, I was told I had to move to Auckland, where she lived. So I thought, *okay! You want me in Auckland, tell me when—and make it easy!* Three months and a very smooth transition later, I was there, and the next stage of my spiritual journey began in earnest.

I started meeting new people, making new friends, doing some new and (what felt like) much bigger spiritual work, and still wondering about the name *A—*. Then, at one of our weekly gatherings, one of the guys mentioned that it was easy to find out what one's Spirit name was. So I had him tell me, there and then.

I practiced what he told me to do, until eventually I heard the name *Amayah*. Weeks later, the name *Grace* dropped in as well, and the two names locked together. It was pronounced the same way as "Amazing

Grace," and I was told that they were one name—that it was *my* name. Later I came to realize that the reason I had to work so patiently to find the name was that I needed that time to raise my vibration, so that I could resonate with the vibration of *AmayahGrace*.

Initially, people would ask me how I got to know my name, and when I would tell them, I could see their eyes glaze over. So after a while, I'd just talk about the work I'd had to do, and would offer to tell them more if they really wanted to know—and none of them did! About a week later, Verna introduced me as AmayahGrace to somebody she knew, who replied "Ah! The Grace of the Divine Mother." This was so big; I felt no sense of connection to it. But as I started to grow into it, I formally changed my name in October 2010, a decade after my life-changing trip to Peru.

Moving to Auckland was a huge leap of faith because I knew so few people there, apart from Verna and those in the spiritual group. I struggled financially—getting the word out about my practice cost money that I didn't have—and after about a year, I went bankrupt. I had to leave where I was living, and would have been homeless but for the generosity of one member of the group who took me in as a boarder. For the next year or so, I managed to survive on the benefit, doing some house- and pet-sitting, and by selling crystals and my healings at weekend fairs. It was tough; I don't seem to remember breathing once during all this time.

Verna had started working with the Ascended Masters to create portal paintings and cards, as well as healing oils, all to help people raise their vibration and facilitate their journey along the path of Ascension. I became one of the first to work with her and the Masters, and it was thanks to this connection, and the cards and oils, that I was able to carry on and start to see possibility again. I particularly remember the impact the Violet Flame oil had on me: within days, I started feeling lighter and freer, and after a couple of weeks, people began commenting on how much younger I was looking.

That was about ten years ago, and during this time, I have raised my vibration from the fourth initiation to the seventh. It is ongoing; the work of clearing and vibration-raising is now simply a part of my life.

During this time, I found out I was on the fifth ray, the Ray of Knowledge, Truth, and Healing. This felt perfect because there have always been things I've *known* and intuitively understood, and because I was doing healing work which felt so natural and effortless. As for the knowledge bit, I never had any inclination to study medicine or to learn more about other healers and their methods—but maybe it was because I trusted that all the knowledge I needed was within me already.

Once I got to the sixth Initiation, however, I moved to the third ray—

the Ray of Unconditional Love and Compassion. And I have my wise, loving, and compassionate Higher Self with me, supporting and guiding me—and making me roar with laughter at some of the things he says. Clearly he's here to help me keep my feet on the ground and to stop me from getting too serious. When I started to become aware of him, I asked him what his name was, eager to hear something highly spiritual or significant—he said his name was Henry Silver. After all, his initials are H.S., which was how I sometimes shortened his title. And only recently have I realized that my own initials, A.G., are the chemical signature for silver. I'm sure he's got some other, more spiritual name, but he won't tell me. I adore him. And as I'm writing this, he tells me, *the feeling's mutual*. I am so blessed.

I now live in the beautiful Bay of Plenty (perfectly named) in a lovely wee home, surrounded by trees and overlooking the estuary. It's my sanctuary, my healing space, for me and for all who come here.

All the work I've been doing for myself has led me to understand that not only is AmayahGrace my name, but that I received it so that I may truly be of service to humanity. I am working with clients to support their own clearing and healing, and I am also working with other seventh initiates, doing what feels like huge work, the implications of which I have no idea. I simply trust where I am guided to go.

Right now, this includes healing and clearing battle sites around the world. I have been part of a group of four seventh initiates, clearing energies trapped in stone circles in the UK (we have recently been told that our involvement is no longer needed, as the sites are now waking themselves up). And on a much smaller (but no less important) scale, for the last year or so, I have been leading groups of seven or eight initiates on the final stage of their journey through the sixth initiation up to the seventh, preparing them for life at the seventh when we truly start to be of service to humanity.

Moreover, I've recently been given a beautiful revelation about my own family. One morning while in the shower (where information and inspiration seem to flow into me with the water), I received a profound understanding of the roles that my brother, my sister, and I chose to embody in this lifetime: the threefold energies of Mind, Body, and Spirit. My (now deceased) brother was an accountant, so he was Mind; before she retired, my sister was a highly skilled physiotherapist, so she is Body; and I am Spirit, with all my client work and Service. As a family we were not particularly religious, nor were we regular churchgoers (apart from the time when we lived in a small village in Devon and my father joined the bellringing team), so this revelation was a delightful surprise. As I shared this with my sister, I was overcome with awe for our now-deceased parents, and their Service in being the vehicles to carry us here. And then they were suddenly there with me—standing in front of me, filled with love and joy and pride for us all.

The results of our choices can be profound, and it's often not until much later that we become aware of the purpose behind our decisions. No wonder they call it the wisdom of hindsight.

I am not the person I was five years ago—or even last year. I have changed, as presumably we all do.

I used to have chronic mild depression; while I was still living in London, I actively imagined ways of committing suicide. When I started meditating and exploring spiritual practices, I became overwhelmed by a vast yearning to go Home (wherever that is). I began connecting to the Masters and using the oils, and shortly after achieving the fifth initiation, I knew that I was not only meant to be here, but that I was actually happy about it.

Shortly after that, I was told I had taken the Bodhisattva vow to be of service to others, "to liberate all sentient beings."

While I am in gratitude for the daily experiences of joy and peace and love that I now have in my life, I am in delight at the prospect of coming back (which is part and parcel of the Bodhisattva vow). I know there are many on this journey who state with great conviction that this is their last lifetime here, and they are *not* coming back; when I tell them that I know that I am, and that I'm really excited about it, they look at me as if I'm crazy.

But I am looking forward to seeing more of the beautiful changes that are starting to come, changes being made to the consciousness of this beautiful blue-green planet of ours, by those who are awake, and by the conscious children, and by the young people who are here now.

And there are so many more beautiful beings, waiting in the wings for their turn.

March, 2019

Chapter Six

Brad Panopoulos

A Journey Led by My Higher Self

"Strive to be in your light, for light cannot cast a shadow"

Brad Panopoulos

Even though I've had encounters off and on throughout my life, I feel that only now, my journey is starting—a journey led by my Higher Self.

At the age of fourteen, I started playing music on an electric bass guitar. This connected me with a family friend from my youth. He and I would chat regularly. I would visit him often, and our conversations grew into those of a spiritual nature. I'm not entirely sure how our talks went down that path, but they did, and it was the start of something that I had no idea would change my life as it has.

This was my introduction into the world of energy and auras, metaphysics and Ascended Masters. Our conversations were multifaceted and not limited to one type of practice or belief system. He would tell me of people that have gone to live with shamans and have studied underneath them. We would talk about abilities, such as the seeing and feeling of the auras of people, animals, trees, plants, and animals.

At the time, I didn't really grasp the concept of Ascension or what an Ascended Master was. However, looking now at what we do know, it's clear that there is limited information on the subject of Ascension, and most people's ideas of it seem to be that of enlightenment. Nonetheless, seeds were planted, as was another seed: my friend had said to me, "I feel this is the last time you're going to be here. You're moving on to whatever it is that comes next . . . whatever that is." This has stuck with me ever since.

So I began to pursue a variety of different practices. I read books on Wicca, shamanism, and gemstones and crystals. I found myself drawn towards druidism, as well as reiki. My friend introduced me to reiki, and I wanted to get into practicing it. He also shared books that I would read.

Yet, during this time in my life, I was also riddled with self-worth issues. Depression, anxiety, and self-destructive patterns took hold of me. I was never big into substances, so this was a path that I luckily avoided despite suffering with my issues. No one ever knew about any of these feelings.

All of this occurred during my late teen years to my mid -twenties. During this period of time, there were many things going on in my life. In August of 2012, my father, whom I only knew a little, died. Also, the relationship I had been in, from which I had two children, came to an end. All of this occurred in the span of a few weeks. I was left to untangle the mess of emotions I suddenly found myself caught up in, as well as a new byproduct of the most recent events: Anger. Lots of it.

Eventually, though, I found myself in another relationship. And about a year later, I started working as a personal trainer. Life was looking up. A lot of what I had been dealing with had lifted. As the months passed, I was able to move through the entanglements quickly—with the exception of how angry I had become.

During this time, I had gotten back into spirituality even more so than before. I started reading books again. I meditated more than I had in years, and every time I'd practice, something in the back of my mind would say, *this is right for me*. I wanted to pursue it more, yet I had no idea what direction to go in. The books I had read in the past didn't seem to call out to me anymore. I needed something different. Later that year, I found myself in a confrontation with someone I had never met. The volcano that had been actively churning inside of me began to erupt. Nothing came of this situation, but it was a clear sign that something needed to change. Where was this path taking me?

Sometime afterwards, I was reintroduced to the idea of the Ascended Masters by my sister in-law. She was always a very spiritually open person and was of great help to chat with when in need. One day she asked me if I knew about the Masters. At the time I knew very little, except through some conversations with my friend and some mention of them in books. But this planted another seed. It sparked my interest, and I couldn't help but do some research. I stumbled around the Internet, going from page to page, reading whatever I could find. By this time I had gotten into binaural beats, (a form of sound therapy that promotes different states of awareness) and a more metaphysical side of spirituality.

Then I found the Alpha Imaging website—or perhaps it found me. The site called out to me, and it was another seed planted; little did I know what this seed would grow into. I immediately took advantage of the free services that were offered, and with that, my pathway to Ascension started.

One morning, while walking to catch the bus to work, I had an *experience*. A flood of feelings, thoughts, and emotions suddenly came through me. Everyone has moments when they feel something coming up—but this was different. It was like I was not only being shown, but *asked* where my anger was going to take me. *What path is this leading you down that you don't see? If you go down that path, then what? Will all your fears become real? Will you go down a path you can't come back from? That is your choice. But there is a different path. There is the Ascension path. You can have this, or you can have what is before you now. This is your choice. We offer you a choice.*

This took place over a few days. Every morning, as I went to catch the bus, I heard: *You can have this! The choice is yours to make!* It was an easy choice really. There wasn't any thinking involved with it. I selected the path I wanted, and with that, an energy moved into my life like a hurricane. A massive shift took place. Looking back at it now, I realize that it had been the Masters offering to take me under their wings and oversee my Ascension.

Not much happened at first. There was no great awakening or opening of my gifts. Over time I learned reiki; Ascension reiki was my first system. There were a few different energy systems that I began learning at the same time. Melchizedek was my Ascension teacher, and clearly, from time to time, there was guidance coming in from him.

I purchased some of the products from the Alpha Imaging site and used them, the protection grid being the first major service I received. I still remember the day I got the grid. It was my birthday. The way I felt that day was just amazing. There was such a change after that. So much more clarity came into my life. As I progressed spiritually, I came to a point where I *felt* this opening taking place: a connectedness, an awareness. There was a lot of knowing. This was around the time of the third initiation and seems to be a common experience among Ascenders. It's a type of enlightenment stage, and it's probably what many in the past have experienced and compared to enlightenment.

But then all of this changed around the fourth initiation. Everything began to unravel—but only so I could be put back together in a much better way.

During this time, I was still in my same relationship. We had a child together, which was my third child. It was a great time, and many things began to shift in my life, but it was also a darker part of my life. All aspects of who I was were coming up for mastery. My life perfectly mirrored everything that I needed to work on. Looking back, I can see that, together, we were going through a darker part of our lives where many aspects of ourselves were being brought up for evaluation.

Throughout 2016, I receiving the healings that I required from the portal. These were lined up week after week. This, in combination with my own guidance, helped me work through the many layers of Self that continued to come up. I was guided to buy a copper meditation pyramid, and this was life-changing for me. At this time, we lived in an apartment, and sitting within it was like stepping into my own sacred space, free from surrounding energies, like taking that first breath of air after being under water for too long. This was a beautiful and much needed addition to my blossoming spiritual life. Also during this time, my passion for making orgonite began to bud (orgonite is a substance made of resin, metals, and quartz that balances and harmonizes bio-energy, chi, or prana, and blocks electro-magnetic frequencies).

A few months after this series of healings from the Ascended Masters portal, I received a personalized healing and passed the fourth initiation. I joined a group of other initiates from the portal. This was the start of a new chapter, and soon after, the start of my service work to the Masters.

About two months after joining the group of initiates, I felt something stirring inside of me. I needed to take things to another level, to take my path even more seriously and be more dedicated. I made a request to my guides, the Masters, my Higher Self, and the universe. I wanted to get things going with what I was supposed to be doing. I made this request on the New Year's Eve of 2016 and wrote it down on paper. I awoke the next day and, again, felt something had shifted. I had felt this shift before; it felt like a movement of energy of a much higher nature. I didn't know it at the time, but it was bringing up my power, the power of Self. My Ascension ray was the blue ray, the Ray of Personal Power versus God's Power.

I was guided to spend time every day on a series of meditations. The one that turned out to be the most important was the Torus technique. I would do the Torus every day, often several times a day. I needed to know it. Then, two days later while on my morning break at work, I had an experience: I saw beams coming at me and connecting to my torus, followed by at least three Masters. Flashes of light and hands surrounded me. I was perplexed by what was going on. My break ended and I went back to work, but the Masters remained with me. For an hour or more, I found myself in a sea of thoughts and emotions. As each wave hit me, I was led down different avenues of thoughts, emotions, and then finally, conclusions: *I had been here before*. I felt differently afterwards, and later discovered that I had been put through a particular lesson that day, a lesson about personal power.

Later that week, a discussion in the initiates group started regarding being of service and what things people are doing for others. I was called upon to lead the group down this path of service work utilizing the group Torus technique. My service to the Masters was to organize the events. Collectively we were coming together for a bigger purpose and that was to provide a platform for the Ascended Masters to work more closely with humanity. Amongst many great ideas that were put forward, I persuaded the group to focus on Mother Earth to provide her with light and healing. A week to the day of my request to do more, I had stepped into a service role with the Masters. The Mother Earth healing was born. Another seed had been planted.

What a great way to be led to your heart space. And, as always, Verna Maruata was there with the right words when I needed them.

The next several months were a whirlwind ride for me. As my service grew and expanded, so did the Masters' guidance and presence in my life. I spent entire days with the Masters' presence around me. From the time I woke up until returning to bed, they were there, or not far off. They were watching and monitoring everything about me: watching to see how I went through my days and how I was in life; my reactions, my thoughts, my emotions, and what I did with them; watching as I was put through tests of self-mastery.

On May 4th, 2016, about six months after joining the initiates group, I passed the fifth initiation. And then, about six weeks later, the sixth initiation was completed. A new chapter had begun, a chapter that would bring my Higher Self into the foreground. But I had one more test that I was unaware of. The numerology of my date of completion of the sixth initiation breaks down into one, which is the beginning of a new cycle.

At the time, I had had no idea that this beautiful service work, along with my personalized healing, had attracted the attention of something darker in nature. By this time, there were many different group Torus events taking place, some with the Ascended Masters, the Elohim, the Angels, and the Cosmic Masters. Physical body healings by the Ascended Masters were also taking place during these events. The group Torus had allowed the Ascended Masters and Beings from the portal to come closer to us in a very different way. But from the tail end of the fifth to just after the sixth initiation, I had started having some dark experiences: experiences of a slight loss of breath combined with tightness in my chest. I could feel some kind of energy around my chest, but it was subtle and had no other indicators with it. I had figured that these were just more Ascension symptoms (since there really is only limited information out there on the topic, let alone about the higher initiations and the physical responses of the body going through these changes). But these escalated quickly after the sixth initiation, and I had an episode that brought me to my knees.

Regardless of my previous issues, I've never had panic attacks. As I knelt, grasping at the floor in my home, my breath taken from me as I hyperventilated, I knew something wasn't right about it; this wasn't merely Ascension symptoms. I'm not too sure how long it lasted, maybe just a minute or two, but after it passed, I was wrecked. I was already in an exhausted state, possibly due to the rate at which I was ascending. This wasn't exactly normal, so I reached out for some advice. It turned out that I had attracted the attention of a "dark being," as it was said to me. This experience seemed like an attempt at possession. But this was more than just that.

This being was attempting to interfere with my Ascension path: to take me away from the Light. But in order for me to continue claiming my Light, I needed to stand in my personal power and keep reaching upwards to my Higher Self. I was being imposed upon by something much bigger than me; an unseen force. Regardless of what I had just experienced, I refused to be bullied away from my Light. The Ascended Masters offered to help me with the part I could not see and remove this Being. I had done my part, in that I did not succumb to fear. A few hours later, I was notified by the Ascended Masters that all was good. This situation was now over with. I stood in my power, and my will had prevailed.

Now, after passing the sixth initiation, I am fully on the blue ray. The blue ray is more than just surrender; it is about power and will. This first ray is about personal power versus God's power and of God's Will over the personal will. This had been a test of my personal power.

Looking back over the years that have passed, I have gained more insights. I now understand with better clarity why I passed from the fourth to the fifth initiations at the rate that I did. It's simple: I surrendered. While it wasn't so easy to do, it was the only way. I was in a position to surrender to God's Will, and that's what I did.

Life seemed to be coming together exactly as I had planned before I started this Ascension path. There were so many things that I wanted to do or create. I wanted to be the master of my own path. But after finding the Ascension path (or perhaps it found me), my life changed dramatically. I was put into a position of complete surrender of my will to the Will of God. And in my surrender, I was asked to walk a different path, a route for which God would lead the way.

Yes, there were many rough patches along this path. Ego would kick up from time to time, and start questioning, *what about this?* And every time this occurred, I was always given the choice to change course, or to continue down God's path. It was tough at times. The tests along the way would require me to dig deeply to overcome them. The tests *still* require this of me, even today. But I continue choosing to walk the road before me. It was in this complete trust and surrender that I managed to move through the fourth initiation so quickly.

And now, as a sixth initiate, I have learned that in surrendering to God's Will, I am, in fact, stepping into my own power. I have learned this through trial by fire. The tests have been immense and have shook me to my core. But, like a blade shaped in the heat of a forge, these experiences have shaped me into who I am today. The blue ray is, in fact, the Warrior Ray.

More than a year has passed since I completed the sixth initiation. My Higher Self is coming more and more into the foreground. Most, if not all, of my past issues are gone. I still have my day job, and am currently working, bit by bit, at building my business in the healing arts (as well as a few other avenues I'm being guided down). With Higher Self in the picture now, energy work has taken on a completely new approach. This, and the addition of some new healing practices, have brought many new changes. My service work with the Masters has expanded again, and I can't help but wonder what the next step will be.

January, 2019

Note: Brad passed the seventh initiation in July, 2019

Chapter Seven

Geri Mason

Over the Rainbow

"I am the light in your heart: the light that illuminates your path. Do you sense a sparkling new world opening up within you?"

My Higher Self

Once, the past seemed like just a random series of situations and events stretching out over the years, and there didn't seem to be any particular sequence or interconnection that I was aware of. Now I see that, all along, I was following an invisible road map with an arrow pointing: *this way*. My soul had already mapped out a path that would gradually unfold, beginning with self-discovery, a spiritual awakening, and eventually, the journey of Ascension. My personal and spiritual growth were essentially interlinked, so my first major challenge was to find myself.

Having paid all my karma, I am off the cycle of rebirth now, and this is my final incarnation. I am on the Ray of My Higher Self, the eighth ray of integration which comprises all rays, the rainbow ray.

This was also my soul ray before I passed the sixth initiation, so it is the continuing theme in my present life.

I was raised in an insecure maternal environment, and overprotected to such an extent that my sense of self was completely entangled with my mum's. It was only in her company that I felt safe and complete. Yet, in my own way, I was happy. Beneath my timid exterior was a cheerful little girl who loved drawing pictures and being surrounded by teddies and dolls. So maybe, at some level, I knew that it was all for a good reason.

But overprotection had far reaching effects. Until my mid-teens, I was almost silent and invisible. Shielded from many aspects of the outside world, my ability to make choices and decisions and form my own opinions was delayed. It took me almost a lifetime to develop a strong sense of my own identity and self-worth. And when I succeeded, it was like a rebirth, a celebration. Now my authentic self is here to stay.

During childhood I was creative and a fast reader, but I struggled to process facts and figures and the situation continued until my early teens. The teachers—and I—assumed that I was intellectually challenged. I left school at sixteen and accepted an office job that wasn't too taxing. Feeling inferior to my friends, I simply resigned myself to my situation even though, deep down, I knew that I was capable of more.

At age 16, I started work for the first time, which was daunting, but I made friends and gradually became more confident. As time went by, I longed to spread my wings; I decided to quit my day job and to spend six weeks abroad, as part of a program to work on the land. At the end of a very long flight from London to the Middle East, I arrived in an environment very different from anything I had ever experienced before. I was free as a bird, and so happy and content that my intended six weeks turned into almost a year.

But as spring turned to early summer, I struggled to cope with the blistering heat. With a heavy heart, I decided to return home. My adventure had come to an end, but it had served its purpose. In less than a year, I had changed from a pleasure-seeking girl making up for lost time into a thoughtful and more mature young woman.

However, I returned home to find that my old friends had moved on. Saturday nights were spent curled up with George Eliot and the Bronte sisters. This didn't do much for my social life (but worked wonders for my vocabulary). "Someday your prince will come," well-meaning relatives assured me. And they were right. Soon I met my Prince Charming on the stairs at work, and later, we were married. We were blessed with a daughter, and then a son: two beautiful souls.

Being a mother led me to discover that constantly giving to others without also giving back to oneself created imbalance. This led me to do more of what gave me pleasure: daily yoga, pranic breathing, and meditation. Then I gathered the courage to take up a part-time degree, and finally proved to myself that I wasn't intellectually challenged after all. I was transformed.

My spiritual awakening soon followed, on the heels of deep sorrow. On a day that started out like any other, the police arrived at my door and gave us the devastating news that my dad had died very suddenly while waiting for a bus on his way to the library. And several days after the shocking news, while walking our puppy down a tree- lined road, I had a vision that stopped me in my tracks. It was a glorious, golden autumn day, and the leaves on the trees were infused with an otherworldly light. Time seemed suspended in a soft, peaceful energy, and I, too, was suddenly filled with peace. I knew at that moment that all was as it was meant to be. We are so much more than the physical body alone.

This was the beginning of my quest for spiritual meaning. Life gradually regained its colour, and eventually I was healed.

I was a city girl, through and through, but we decided to leave the pollution behind and move to a rural area where the children could breathe fresh air. What a culture shock! As I surveyed the muddy fields and only one small grocery store, it was like leaving civilization behind. But I grew to love the energy of the countryside. I was drawn to wildlife, with its pure and innocent soul, and was in awe of the way a Higher Power always manages to guide us to the right place at the right time.

The peace and quiet of the countryside was my inspiration, but it never succeeded at defining every aspect of my life. With both children at school, the days were long and increasingly unsatisfying. This caused me to re-evaluate my life, and I became a volunteer with Samaritans, a twenty-four-hour helpline for people who were in crisis or suicidal. Soon I decided to take my listening skills further, and began four years of training as a therapeutic counselor. Self-development was an integral part of my learning, which paved the way for the much deeper self-awareness needed for Ascension.

On an overcast autumn day, I had a powerful spiritual experience while sitting at the kitchen table writing an essay. I paused, trying to decide what to say, and noticed that colours seemed brighter, and that the rhythm of my breathing had changed. It was slower, almost imperceptible. The room had filled with the tranquil, loving energy of my guides, and it suddenly occurred to me to write down whatever came into my mind. The result was two pages of gentle and uplifting words.

I had channeled for the first time. I was ecstatic and wanted to tell the world. But who would believe me? So, instead, I kept it a precious secret, tucked safely away in my heart. Getting to know my guides and building a close and loving bond with them was an amazing new beginning, and the prelude to my Ascension in this lifetime. But the smooth flow of my spiritual progression was interrupted when I started to overthink my experience and tried to analyze it. Nothing made sense to me, and I entered into a dark night of the soul. I was in a lonely place but when I re-emerged, my faith and trust were stronger than ever before. My guides had suddenly reappeared and I was filled with an energy of love, peace and light. From that moment, I knew for certain that the truth - my truth - was in my heart, and not in the analytical thoughts going around in my head. The dark night of the soul had ended, heralding in a deeper spirituality and a more peaceful heart and mind.

Later that year, I graduated and felt guided to work at a local hospice with clients who were bereaved or terminally ill. The work was deep and rewarding, but emotionally draining. Yet I always felt supported by the loving and peaceful energy that surrounded me. Clients often discussed their spiritual beliefs and how they imagined heaven would be. I was powerfully aware that listening and the spoken word could be profoundly healing, and I tried to make a difference in ways that were beyond the physical. When I felt it was time to move on from my work at the hospice, I decided to rest and recharge. I was ready to embark on a new path and focus on my spirituality.

For almost as long as I can remember, I longed to have healing hands. And when the time was right, my prayers were answered. My guides helped me to develop my healing gift, which did much good in my service at the hospice, and which I still cherish today, as it continues to evolve. But it seemed that my guides were with me for a specific purpose, and they gradually began to stand back once I left the hospice, to make way for a new phase of my life. Their departure left a gaping hole, and I sorely missed them. I was completely lost. I made a half-hearted attempt to find new spiritual meaning via Google. Suddenly a website appeared as if by magic. My discovery of Alpha Imaging was a beacon of light. It was life changing.

Ascension and the Ascended Masters were new to me, and every day, I read as much on the website as my eyes could cope with in one sitting. I was fascinated by everything I learned. From the other side of the world, I met Verna Maruata and Waireti, who work with the Ascended Masters in their portal in New Zealand. And I discovered the portal store, with healings and products infused with the Masters' energy to help accelerate our Ascension. It was like entering a different world, with more clarity and meaning than ever before.

I learned that I was somewhere between the second and third initiation, and that there was a rainbow above the crown of my head (how I wished I had been blessed with the gift of seeing). This meant that I had incarnated onto the eighth ray. My other rays included the fifth (green) ray of Healing, Truth, and Knowledge (perfect!). This was my personality ray. Master Hilarion was my temporary Ascension teacher, but later, White Tara stepped in.

Life was relatively quiet, with only subtle changes. But I had become increasingly sensitive to negative energy, with intense headaches and pains in various parts of my body. The protection grid gave me my life back. Then I went through a phase of channeling at every opportunity, and became increasingly ambitious. Channeling Plato and Socrates sounded like an exciting idea, and very soon, the pages of my notepad were filled with words—but whomever it was that I had channeled, it definitely *wasn't* the Ancient Greek philosophers. This was my introduction to astral pretenders, and it was a lesson well learned.

My next reading showed that I had passed the fourth initiation, having paid eighty percent of my karma. I was invited to join a large group of fellow initiates from different parts of the world, kindred spirits whose friendship and support have since spurred me on. It felt like being embraced in a warm, group hug. Despite bizarre Ascension symptoms that came and went, and old friendships falling away because we had less in common, I loved being on the fourth initiation. It was a very special time for me.

I had always felt a heart connection with the angels, and at this point, they entered my life in a new and dramatic way. I began to hear singing: beautiful, pure voices, sometimes male and at other times female, often singing together in harmony. It seemed like the singing and music varied according to the category of angels. At times, it sounded ethereal and higher than any human voice could reach, or it was sweet sounding and accessible with an almost human quality. Sometimes the singing was like a cathedral choir in the living room. At other times, it came from the sky and was awe-inspiring in its power. The music was played on instruments I couldn't define because they were not of this world. The closest comparison would be cellos, flutes, pipes, and guitars filled with divinity. The effect was always the same. The singing and music worked on my heart and entire aura, and it was deeply healing. I wish the whole world could experience this profound healing of heart and mind, and then maybe there could be peace on Earth.

Several days before passing the fifth initiation, I felt the powerful and loving presence of my Ascension teacher, White Tara. I sensed she was asking if I was ready. Having moved forward at a snail's pace and feeling like I was the longest serving fourth initiate on the planet, I was definitely ready! Then I noticed that the Violet Flame oil had stopped working on my chakras. This suggested that all my karma was cleared and that I had passed the fifth initiation. I was so excited! Over the coming weeks and months, waves of light, at increasing intensities, entered my heart. I felt more spiritually connected, and increasingly loving and accepting towards myself and others. I received confirmation from Verna that not only had I passed the fifth initiation but had already begun the sixth. This was completed in a few weeks, and I vividly remember my feelings when I was given the good news: immense joy and gratitude, bewilderment and disbelief. *Am I dreaming?* No! It was real!.

I would have loved to spend the day in quiet contemplation, absorbing the higher intensity of light. But we had already arranged to meet family for a pub lunch. My aura felt soft, like it was wrapped in satin. I felt detached, as if I was observing everything from a distance. I was surprised that I could communicate as normal, and I'm sure no one noticed that anything was different. Lying in bed that night, I was being heavily grounded, and my feet felt like they had weights attached to them. I had the sensation of my legs being stretched, and I felt much taller (although it was just a sensory illusion). The following day, I felt more grounded and was already acclimatizing to a higher vibration.

On the sixth initiation, the Masters stepped back as teachers and I began to connect with my Higher Self, to develop a relationship with this loving and mysterious stranger who I couldn't wait to get to know. I sensed his sparkly energy in my heart and around my aura, and I felt calm and peaceful. I began to see little rainbows in unlikely places: paper towels, the kitchen sink and kettle, even on the banister at McDonald's! I was slow to catch on, and kept asking my Higher Self to show me the colour of my new ray. After several weeks of asking, I was lying in bed and my heart and third eye were filled with intense energy. I clearly saw rainbow colours passing slowly in front of my closed eyes. I already felt bonded with the eighth ray, and I was over the moon when it was confirmed that my ray was still the same.

Now, just over half way to the seventh initiation, my Higher Self is guiding me along a continuous path of insight and growth. Have I achieved what was required of me in those earlier days? Yes, I believe so. I had often wondered why my soul had chosen the challenges of my early life for me; now my Higher Self has given me the answer: It was so that I could create myself anew. In keeping with the eighth ray, my purpose was to refine and integrate any remaining rough edges, to heal and balance aspects of myself that were still disconnected. To do this, I needed to change the way I perceived myself and the world around me. At a conscious level, I wasn't aware of any of this at the time; however, on a soul level, I clearly realized that there was something important that I needed to do.

The outcome of this journey is that I am in a state of balance, less reactive, and more loving and accepting towards self and others. Old insecurities continue to fade away. I have an understanding of how all the rays influence my journey, and there is still much for me to learn. As for the eighth ray in its entirety, it is a mystery to me. I can only understand it through my senses and what is in my heart. To me, it radiates immense love and compassion, tranquility and unity with all that is. Slowly the qualities of the ray are becoming a part of me, and this will increase as I continue to ascend.

Being in service is an important part of our Ascension, and I realize that this can be fulfilled in many different ways. Even a smile or a listening ear can make a difference, and a recent experience highlighted this for me. As I waited in a long queue of people that didn't seem to be moving, my impatience mounted. Then I noticed an elderly man in front of me who was having difficulty forming his words. I beamed love into his heart, and he turned to me and smiled. Wow, the power of love. We can do so much good in even the smallest ways. Love is everything.

The portal cards and other Ascended Master treasures are still on the bedside table. They are a reminder of the Masters' love and healing, and of my incredible journey from the moment Verna Maruata and Waireti came into my life. The healing shawl is wrapped around my shoulders at night, and my protection grid is permanently in place. Ascension isn't always easy, but I wouldn't change it for the world. Right now, it's like the Magical Mystery Tour!

I'm uncertain where my path will take me, but I know that I will go forward, hand-in-hand, with my loving and wise Higher Self, and He will lead the way.

February, 2019

Note: In August, 2019, Geri passed the seventh initiation.

Chapter Eight

Simi Ahuja, M.D.

A Trail of Love

"From the depths of a woman's heart arises an ocean of courage, faith and trust. The wave of which can transform the world."

Simi Ahuja

I am an American M.D. I am often encouraged to mention this credential to lend credibility to my story. However, this journey of Ascension has humbled me, and has led me to the belief that certifications from the external world are of limited value. For me, the greatest of all accomplishments is embodying my Higher Self. This is my purpose, my mission, and my vision. They are all in alignment.

First and foremost, I AM. From that place of I AM-ness, I give the gift of healing through my practice of Mind-Body Medicine. In order to practice from the depth of my being-ness, I have learned that this work is about commitment, about persistence, and about vigilance to your higher calling.

While this is a journey of love, courage, trust, and faith, it will challenge you to the core. Make no mistake about that. It will unravel the web of the ego. It will disempower the personality and lift your Self up, all at the same time. You will have challenges, and you will be tested along the way to see how strong your resolve is, to see if you are really ready for the power that you contain and the responsibility that comes with your power.

The purpose of our incarnation is our evolution. We choose certain lessons that help us to evolve, even before our incarnation. Either we can stay victimized or we can use these lessons to transcend and ascend, and claim our destiny. There is no wrong choice here. One will keep us stuck in our suffering; the other will lift us up from it. It's when the motivation to get out of our suffering exceeds the fear of shining our light that we go through this journey in a conscious way. Neither approach is wrong, as we will all transcend our suffering one day. It is just a matter of time.

As I sit back and reflect on this journey, I can see that when we act from a place of unconsciousness, much damage is caused. Not just to our loved ones, but to our beautiful planet, the universe, and even galaxies, as the ripple effect of our thoughts and actions are vast and far reaching—we are that powerful. I have also realized how deep these wounds really are, and how they have become an intricate part of every fibre of our being. It is what makes us who we are. It is the reason we act the way we do. It is reflected in the big and the little things alike, such as how we relate to one another, how we eat, how we think, how we walk, how we speak, how we drive, and so on. These wounds become a blueprint for the physical body. If we try to heal our physical body without healing our wounds, it is like trying to build a new modern building using an old and outdated building blueprint. It simply does not work.

A TRAIL OF LOVE

If you want to heal the physical body, you must first heal the wounded inner child. And when we heal this wounded child, our physical bodies will also heal (unless the trauma occurred at the physical level). One cannot happen without the other.

I was born in India to an orthodox Sikh family. In India, the birth of a female is seen as a bad omen, because women are seen as money pits and lesser beings then men. In the 1960's it was, and still is, a common practice to give dowry. Often the poor will pawn all of their assets in order to collect the needed money for a dowry for their daughters. If they don't, there is a great chance that their daughters will be burned alive after marriage for not bringing enough dowry with them. This makes giving birth to a daughter a grief process rather than a celebratory one. Since we are naturally empathic as souls, this limiting and damaging belief impacts us even in the womb. We feel it even before we are born, leading to a sense of insecurity during this tender time of our development. So trauma began even before I was born, preparing me to fulfill my destiny.

My parents were poor, and we had to live with my father's sister in order to make ends meet. My aunt had four children, two sons and two daughters. My aunt's children were significantly older than me, and the daughters lived with their grandmother. My dad, my mom, my brother, and I all lived with my aunt and her two sons in a small three-room house above a bazaar in New Delhi, India.

Starting at the age of six, my two cousins began to sexually molest me. My mom would leave me in their care after school while she went to visit her family, who lived just a few miles away. My cousins would take advantage of the trust my mom placed in them. They would sexually abuse me in my moms' absence. This went on from the ages of six to twelve. It only stopped because our family immigrated to the U.S. when I was twelve years old, in 1982.

The move to America was both a blessing and a curse because one form of trauma was replaced by another. We moved to the south side of Milwaukee where there was very little cultural diversity. I became lost in this American culture that had no culture. Because of the sexual abuse, I had very low self-worth and was dissociated from my body. Then I was thrown into this environment where I was teased and harassed for who I was. This was not only embarrassing but also very confusing. The family values, the religious beliefs, and the way of life were so very different from what I had known while growing up in India. So I began to question everything that I had been taught up to that point. I was utterly and hopelessly lost.

In time, I began to rebel against my family by lying to them. The sad thing was that I never got caught for my lies, which made me feel invisible and uncared for. In many ways, this validated my sense of low self-worth, strengthening the belief that I was unlovable. I now know that this is where my trust issues as an adult stem from.

Research has shown that brain development stops at the time of a trauma. The normal cognitive processes of the brain develop at about age six. My brain never developed properly, leading to cognitive dysfunction. This meant that I did not have processes in place to make good decisions, which led to poor performance in school and other areas of life. The belief that I was invisible truly made me think that regardless of my performance in school, no one would see it.

My mom was big on education, so I was sent to college. But I wasn't a good student in college either. Then my best friend got into one of the top medical schools in the country. This was a great awakening for me, as I was shocked that she had not only gotten into medical school, but she had landed a spot in one of the most prestigious medical schools in the country. I had assumed that, since we hung out together, she must have been as stupid as I was—like attracts like. But seeing what she had accomplished made me suddenly become aware of my own potential, that I, too, had the intelligence and the worth to go to medical school.

I, too, had the potential to become the healer that I had always wanted to be, but had been, thus far, unwilling to admit to myself, for fear of failure.

When I was in India, I had dreamt about being a mystical healer. I saw and heard about many different healers, including a woman who would instantly manifest things from her hands, right in front of my seven-year-old eyes. From that moment onwards, I knew that that was what I wanted to do one day. I was in awe of her gift.

But my dream was lost while living in America, because there was no such thing as a healer there. Or if there was, no one talked about it. It almost seemed like it was a taboo subject. And so, as a way to survive, I began to think like the Americans did. I started to believe that mysticism was silly, that it was non-existent. I abandoned my dream of becoming a healer—until my friend's acceptance to medical school re-kindled my soul. Her achievement gave me the courage to pursue my childhood dream. So I worked hard in my last year of college and achieved very good grades. This was proof to myself of my brilliance.

Also in that last year of college, I met someone who wanted to date me. At first I said no; but after much persistence on his part, I finally gave in. I knew that if I dated him, I would end up marrying him. I realize now that I had no feelings for him—but, being an empath, I picked up on his feelings for me and ran with it. Unfortunately, lies, manipulation, and deceit were the foundation of our relationship.

I knew that my parents would never approve of our relationship, so in order to date him I lied to my parents yet again. But one day my brother found out; he asked me to tell my parents, and that if I didn't, he would. This was an act of love that I am grateful for, but of course, just as I imagined, my parents strongly disapproved of him. My parents were thinking of an arranged marriage for me, but the concept of an arranged marriage was terrifying. I wasn't a virgin, and I was afraid that when I married my husband, he would know this and would somehow expose me, which would be disgraceful to my family. I began to feel safe in my invisibility. I felt a lot of shame at not being a virgin.

And so, after my last class in college, I ran away from home with my then boyfriend, leaving my family worried and in pain at the loss of their daughter. However, I truly believed that no one would even notice I was gone. We moved to an entirely different state where no one knew us and started a new life. I worked odd jobs, such as an announcer at a local farmer's market or a cashier at a franchised grocery store, earning minimum wage. We were making just enough money to pay the rent. But as I worked these jobs, I knew deep inside that I was meant to do something more. My soul continued to push me to go to medical school. So one day I gave in to the nagging, and fortunately, I was able to study medicine.

My state of mind was not optimal, and by this time, I had a one-and-a-half-year-old daughter. The odds that I was going to make it through medical school were abysmal. One of the biggest things I had going for me, however, was Grace. The Grace of God was my anchor during those challenging times. It not only helped me survive medical school—it helped me thrive.

People who experience sexual trauma at an early age more often end up in a psych ward than in a medical school. When I reflect on my time in medical school, I am astonished that I made it through. I had to listen to each lecture three times, and read each chapter three times, in order to understand the material. This wasn't because I was stupid; it was because I was so dissociated from my body, due to all the trauma. I still did not feel safe enough in my body to remain there for any length of time.

Eventually, my hard work paid off and I graduated from medical school with honours and nearly perfect grades. However, once I graduated and started to practice as a physician, I quickly realized that this was not what I had wanted to do after all. I wanted to be a *healer*, not a factory doctor. Yet nothing I learned in medical school prepared me to be the healer I so longed to be. I felt frustrated, stuck, and isolated. Nor was I happy with my home life. I had lost all connection with my parents and the rest of the family. My husband would not speak to me for months at a time. It was clear I was not the mother, the wife, the daughter, the doctor, or the healer that I so wished to be.

That is when I went in search of God, for deep down, I knew that nothing less than a higher power could straighten out the mess that I had made out of my life. Intellectually, I knew that God was within me; yet I did not know how to look for Him. So I went in search of God outside of me, hoping that someone would help to point the finger inwards, so I could find the Divinity within me.

I began to take spiritual classes and read spiritual books. I also did the lessons in A Course in Miracles (ACIM). I found a teacher who taught me the art of looking within. When I began the journey within, I realized that the healer I yearned to be was already within me, but that I needed to first let go of the grievances, the blame, the shame, the resentment, the jealousy, and other negative thoughts in order to tap into the power that I had as a Divine Being. The more I released, the more I realized the power of the mind to heal the physical body. This was in alignment with the teaching of ACIM when Jesus said, "An illness is a sign of anger in the mind."

And I started to wonder: if an illness is a sign of anger in the mind, then why don't we practice this principle in Western medicine to help all those who are suffering?

While taking one of my spiritual classes, I came across a gentleman from Germany who had undergone three surgeries for a hernia repair that was not healing. His team of doctors told him that he could expect the wound to heal in about three to four months. From experience, I knew that seromas take a long time to heal. They told him that if the wound healed, it would leave a disfiguring scar and he would need surgery to repair it. And if the wound *didn't* heal, he would need a fourth surgery anyway. He also shared with me that he had been married for fifty years but had been estranged from his wife for the last twenty of them. They lived in the same house as roommates. That is when the download came to me that he needed to heal his relationship with his wife in order for the wound in his body to heal. I shared this information with him and he decided to love his wife unconditionally. Within two days, he rekindled his relationship with his wife, and within ten days, his wound healed entirely, without leaving a disfiguring scar.

This situation helped me realize the immense power of the mind to heal the physical body. So I began to apply this principle to myself.

To my amazement, I was able to heal my cognitive brain dysfunction. Before I knew it, I began to make sound judgements about my life. I had the courage to leave my husband of twenty years, and I left a job that no longer served my purpose. In that letting go, I was gifted with a beautiful life filled with peace, harmony, and abundance.

Yet there was something still missing. Even as a sixth level initiate, and just about three-quarters of the way through my Ascension initiations, I still felt like I was not the person I wanted to be externally. Yes, internally there had been a great shift—yet I felt that was not reflected in my outward persona. This disconnect, admittedly, left me confused about the Ascension process. I was confused at this high level of disconnect between my physical persona and my inner vibration.

Then I was given the crucial, missing piece for my evolution. I learned that if the trauma happens at the level of the physical body, then it needs to be healed at the level of the physical body as well. Our physical body holds onto emotions, just like our emotional body does. Our body is like an inner child; it needs the same loving care and attention that our inner children do. I recognized that I needed to purify the physical body just as I had purified the emotional and the mental bodies. While clearing the subtle bodies helped to heal the physical body, I needed to work directly with the physical in order to release the emotions that were blocking the flow of energy in the nadis. This flow is vital to our survival. And I realized that I couldn't think, or even emote, my way out of that physical process.

To heal that last part of me, I was guided to go to Colombia. The missing piece had several components. First and foremost, I needed the energetic support of the Goddess energy, which was provided by that magical place. To help me integrate this Goddess energy into my physical being, I was guided to practice tantric yoga. I began to see changes emerging in my physical body immediately with the practice of this yoga. I was able to assimilate these energies further with the assistance of a tantric sex therapist.

When I first started the practice of tantric yoga, I felt huge feelings of helplessness resurfacing. This allowed me to understand the helplessness that I had been feeling every moment of everyday but could never figure out where it was coming from. I realized that this was the same helplessness that I had felt when I laid in the bed while my cousins molested me. My body was frozen and my soul dissociated, leaving me feeling numb.

The more I practiced tantric yoga, the more I was able to release that feeling of helplessness. The sex therapist helped me assimilate these energies so I could feel whole again.

Within a couple of weeks of arriving in Colombia, I saw my body begin to transform like I had never seen before. I began to see glimpses of the empowered woman that resided within me and who yearned to come out. I began to realize that throughout my life, I had wanted my sexuality to be invisible, which gave me the appearance of a woman who was meek, timid, and disempowered.

Why it is so important for us to heal our sexuality, whether we experience abuse or not? This discussion is long overdue. There are many stigmas, taboos, and myths associated with our sexuality, making it difficult to have a heartfelt, authentic discussion about this subject. It is time for us to have this discussion unapologetically and uncensored, instead of shoving it under the rug and hoping it goes away. Because that is where our healing lies.

Why did I work so hard to heal this part of me? Because I wanted to no longer be ashamed of my sexual desires. I wanted to live life to the fullest, and that involved embracing *all* of me, including my sexuality. Our sexuality is who we are. Our sexuality is our power. Our sexuality is our creativity. Our sexuality is our manifesting ability. Instant manifestation requires our sexual energy to flow at its optimum. The Divine energy is orgasmic, leading us to a state of ecstasy. It is our birthright. It is not something to be judged, oppressed, and boxed up. It is an expression of love.

The key component to harvesting the power of our sexuality is our heart. There has to be an energetic connection between our heart and our sexual organs. Otherwise, the sex becomes animalistic rather than a sacred expression of love. It leaves us with a feeling of emptiness rather than fulfillment. The energetic connection between the heart and our womb space is what allows us to experience and connect with the universe in an entirely different and direct way, leading to a feeling of Oneness with All.

Unfortunately, this connection is severed through various means, including conditioning that goes along with child rearing and, of course, with sexual abuse. But the flow can be regenerated through tenacity, resolve, and assistance from the universe.

For me, I was able to heal this deep wound through tantric yoga practice, in combination with somatic and tantric sex therapy and years of unrelenting inner child work. And something else that also helped me open my heart was, undeniably, the spirit of San Pedro. Never having experienced any sort of drugs in the past, including smoking or drinking, I was not sure what to expect from plant medicines when the spirit of San Pedro called to me. The ceremony was intense, magnificent, and extremely therapeutic, all at the same time. Done with the right intention, it creates magic. The healing occurred at both a personal level and at the level of the soul group. As a result, the heart opening was palpable in a room full of thirty people. Personally, it helped me open up my heart, especially to men; it allowed sexual energy to flow again so that I could express my desires freely, instead of hiding behind shame and guilt and wearing a cloak of invisibility. Once I had healed this part of me, I no longer needed to binge eat in order to fulfill my desire for pleasure—I stopped looking for sexual pleasure in food. I rediscovered my sovereign spiritual right to be able to express my sexuality, a right that I finally came to see as mine just as much as everyone else's.

It is time to relinquish limiting beliefs that tether us to self-imposed restrictions. When we hide behind shame and guilt, it leaves us to live an unfulfilled and empty life, which we try to fill with alcohol, food, and other drugs that lead to a myriad of diseases and suffering. This is all because we lack the willingness and the courage to explore this very hidden part of ourselves. It is time for us to shine our light brightly, sexuality and all. It is time for us to claim our sacred sexuality. It is time for us to step into our destinies.

This passage into Ascension has been nothing short of amazing, as it has taken me full circle and has prepared me to be the healer that I was meant to be. What continues to fascinate me about this whole Ascension process is how my training began from the very moment I was conceived. Since then, every moment of my life has been in service to preparing me for my destiny. This journey has given me the courage to bring forth a new paradigm of practicing medicine. It was all part of the Divine plan to give me the warrior training that I needed in order to bring about this shift in medicine. It has provided me with the necessary gifts and tools that can assist with changing the blueprint of the physical body by getting to the root cause of an illness.

As a doctor, I witness so much suffering and illness, and feel that even with all of the state-of-the-art equipment and evidence-based medicine, we have not even begun to scratch the surface of how to prevent a disease that consumes our being and leaves us devoid of life. I only began to heal once I began to search outside the box of conventional medicine. As you can see from my story, all the components that I needed to heal my life were not found in a doctor's office or in a hospital. Nor were they found in any church or religious group. They were found within my heart. It's when I listened to my heart that a trail was carved out for my healing. Unsurprisingly, it was also the trail that led the way back to my heart.

This journey is what makes me so passionate about Mind-Body Medicine. What I have discovered is that a disease is just a symptom of a lack of self-love and acceptance. Once we fully love all parts of ourselves, including our shadow aspect and our sexuality, we can truly love others and our world. I feel our sexuality is perceived as the darkest of the shadows within us, and it took the greatest courage for me to accept this part of myself. I am finally able to claim my life fully.

And I have a passion to help others live their lives to the fullest. I have techniques and tools to share with others so that they, too, can live a life free of suffering. But the most precious gift I share with others is my Higher Self, who is the healer within me and is able to shine the light on the healer within you. But the journey is yours to embark upon, for those who dare to look outside the box and are willing to do their inner work.

Most importantly, this journey has helped me realize that from the depths of a woman's heart can arise an ocean of courage, faith, and trust. My story is not just mine. It is a representation of the collective journeys of the Divine Feminine that lies within each and every one of us.

This story is written with the intention to inspire and connect you to the Divinity that is within you. I have now realized that the God within me that I went in search of is my Higher Self, who cherishes and loves me unconditionally. *She* is the one I was searching for all my life. I am currently at the sixth initiation; my Higher Self is on the third ray of Unconditional Love. The magic of this journey lies in its unfoldment. As we travel along the way, we are truly given that which we need to fulfill our destiny.

This is a nomadic journey like no other. Savour every moment of it. May this inspire you to step forward into your own personal nomadic journey, and to carve a new trail for those who are behind you.

February, 2018

Note: In August, 2019, Dr Ahuja passed the seventh initiation.

Chapter Nine

Luz Victoria Winter

From Caterpillar to Butterfly

*"In the world of caterpillars and butterflies,
a butterfly has earned its right to fly"*

Luz Victoria Winter

As I began this writing, I could not help but think of practical information that I could provide the reader with. I appreciate my spiritual journey, but how is it applicable to the reader? I could indulge myself with stories about mystical feats and experiences that might be entertaining, but might also have you question my sanity. So I have opted to write in a practical manner with splashes of mystical experiences, intentionally not elaborating on what may be outlandish to some, entertaining to others, but also very private to me.

Before modern Ascension, the path to be of light with God (enlightenment) required an extreme commitment and drastic measures. There was a curriculum that various monks followed, involving surrender and complete trust in the teacher, master, or guru. Many books are available that describe their journeys. There were specific patterns involved with this level of commitment. Much of it involved isolation, pain and suffering, and release from the material world. It was the classic journey to enlightenment, regardless of your faith. Am I enlightened after a similar journey? Enlightenment is not a fixed state; it is an ongoing process. This is my journey as it has unfolded.

As a child, I lived in my own world, filled with a vivid imagination. I believed that there was more to my life than that which I could see. When my mother told me that Santa Clause, the Tooth Fairy, and the Easter Bunny did not exist, I was devastated. *Is this all that there is? You mean there is no magic around me?* Life without those figures seemed dull and lifeless.

As I grew older, my quest for something more than this three-dimensional human existence was rekindled when I started reading about angels, beings from other dimensions, and yes, Jesus, who was accessible without the use of a third party. I began experimenting in church and found that I could contact Jesus and other beings that were beyond the three-dimensional eye. I learned that when I was in contact with the right frequency of light, I felt an immense sense of peace. It was a sense of peace that filled my heart and brought me more satisfaction than anything in the material world. The material world made me feel unworthy.

I was living in Santa Fe, New Mexico, when I first began the early stages of my spiritual exploration. That period in my life brought many physical guides that were willing to provide me with all sorts of services. I now refer to this as my Spiritual Shopping Stage. I explored various religions and forms of energy work, and also explored tools such as crystals, tarot cards, and astrology. There were healers all around me that were willing to heal me—at an expensive price. Some of the guides were authentic, but others were not what they presented themselves to be. I learned at that time that being on a spiritual path was confusing. *Who do I believe?*

It was during that time that spiritual materialism was introduced to me. Money was needed in order to buy products and services that would lead to enlightenment. This concept seemed odd because money was not needed for the earlier monks and saints that obtained enlightenment. Despite the contradiction, I enjoyed being a part of the New Age crowd. We talked the same language and bought many of the same products. What troubled me about this stage was that there was no growth. I was having experiences and learned about a healthier way of living, but my inner wounds and outer drama continued. Unhealthy patterns of thinking continued. Mystical experiences could be twofold: they could provide the incentive to further one's spiritual understanding, or they could become addictive. One could have continuous mystical experiences without growing internally. In retrospect, however, I can see how this stage was significant in my life, as it helps me relate to many who are going through the Spiritual Shopping Phase today.

After a period of shopping around, I was guided to find a spiritual role model. In my mind at that time, I was searching for a female version of the Dalai Lama. A week later, a full-page picture of an Indian saint appeared in our local newspaper. I cut out the picture and put it on the refrigerator. When a male acquaintance visited me, I told him that that was the woman that I needed to meet. He told me that he knew where her ashram in Santa Fe was located, and that he would take me to her.

When I saw Amma in person, my recognition of her was instantaneous—I had known her well from a past life, as I later discovered. As a person who grew up Catholic, I didn't understand the specifics of Hinduism; however, I knew that my relationship with this woman was unique. At that time, I had to create my own limited definition of what she was to me, and that was a Divine Mother.

I continued to see her once or twice a year when she came to the United States, for about four years. I now call this stage my Seduction Stage with the spiritual guru. I learned more about the rituals involved with Hinduism while gaining friendships with others who shared my commitment to this spiritual teacher, Amma, all the while maintaining my life as a classroom teacher. I was able to blend my work and family life with my new spiritual community. My spiritual journey at this time was more focused than before, but was still non-transformational. In retrospect, I now know that I needed to clear a few loose ends before I could become her disciple.

Four years later, my guru asked me, "Do you want to be a householder? Or a spiritual person?" The question posed by my guru seemed contradictory at first—why did it have to be *either/or*? Why can't a householder be a spiritual being? What did she mean by "spiritual person"?

What I *did* know was that a householder was a person that lived in the everyday world, working, having children, and living the life that most people in my country did. And so, without even knowing the specifics of what it entailed, I gave her my response: I wanted to live a spiritual life.

Soon after my response, my life dramatically changed. I left a householder relationship, left my job as a special education teacher, and dropped down the rabbit hole.

The best way to describe this next stage that commenced is as one of preparation for more intense spiritual training. At this point, I learned that I have healing abilities, and other abilities that would later become strengthened. I connected with a controversial group and began an intensive study of energy work. Our whole world was that of energy work from different perspectives, including Eastern, Western, New Age, and applications of ancient energy work techniques. We travelled around the world, focusing on major energy points. This level of training lasted for about three years. I wasn't sure where this work was leading me, and I had no idea that there were still future stages ahead, but I knew that I was following a prescribed program supported by my guru.

The next chapter in my Ascension journey involved leaving the group that I had been travelling with in Egypt and Greece, and travelling on alone to India to stay in my guru's ashram. I didn't know what to expect in India; I only knew that I was to "stay for quite a while", as my guru had instructed me when I had last seen her in the United States. So I had packed for what I had believed to represent "a stay for quite a while," and ventured to the unknown land of my guru.

It is commonly said that when one arrives in India, one is immediately hit with exotic smells and visions of colour; it is true. I was in awe of my surroundings as I was transported to Amma's ashram. The movie and book *Eat, Pray, Love* by Elizabeth Gilbert accurately describes the early stages of that period in my life. I was quickly indoctrinated into ashram life in India. I dressed in white Indian clothing, learned the rituals of the faith, and did my best to blend in with other ashramites. I travelled with Amma around India as she met crowds of people, providing them with spiritual talks and the famous Amma hug. The tour was grueling, but I was transforming. Humility, surrender, trust, and love began to override me on a level I never knew existed. I did not know it at the time, but I was clearing a great deal of karma, and thus suffered from various ailments and bizarre circumstances that were not pleasant. By the end of the six month visit, I had learned how to be an Amma disciple. This was the Boot Camp Training Phase.

When I returned to the United States, I was different. My values had changed, and minimalism became important. I was praying, chanting, and meditating on a regular basis. And when I reconnected with Amma when she came to the West Coast, I was no longer the awkward Westerner—I was a part of the Amma system. I knew when to bow, how to sit, how to dress, and how to behave around the guru.

My energy work training had become more specific. Amma supported my continued energy work as I worked with Shiva, Krishna, Lakshmi, Ganesh, and other Indian deities. I had the gift of direct communication with the Indian deities, and with Amma. My past life gifts with energy work were strengthened.

I did not know that my journey would grow in intensity. After a few months in the United States, I was called back to India, but this time, away from the ashram. I was to travel around India by myself, going to various Amma programs throughout the country. I had never travelled alone internationally. In retrospect, this new period forced me to grow inward and to trust my guidance. I was a hermit that lived in the cave of hotels. I had little communication with people, but was able to have my physical needs met in a safe manner. I received direction from Amma and my guides (who I would later come to identify as my Ascended Masters) through different programs of instruction. It was a magical time, when I personally experienced the synchronicity of following my inner guidance and watching the impossible occur. I learned during this stage that if I followed God's will, the pieces would come together, and I would get what I needed, when I needed it. It was a marvelous way to exist.

Trust, faith, and surrender did not provide me with a road map to the future. I needed to master the art of living in the moment. I learned to relish the moment and know that the moment would eventually lead to my next step. I was forced to tune inward to know what to do and where to go. And then I expanded my travels, moving around the world by myself and seeing Amma at various programs around the globe. I was a mysterious figure that sat in the front row of her programs, and seemed to follow different rules than those around her.

Each person that is born into this world is of a predominant soul ray. This ray influences our path to God. My ray at that time was the Ray of the Goddess, and that of Devotion to God, and eventually, the God Within. At the time, others had strong opinions of me, questioning why I was treated differently. I was a controversial figure during this period. But now I understand why my guru insisted that I dress in beautiful saris while those around me wore white. I understand why my spiritual program was different from the spiritual programs of those disciples around me. Much of this setup was to help clear karma, and also to follow my spiritual program of devotion to the Goddess. During that time, I learned to completely focus on my instruction without being offset by the projection of others. I learned to have faith in my energy work abilities. I followed a curriculum that involved tests that demonstrated mastery of certain concepts before I could move to the next level of instruction. Unlike my previous stages, I was transforming into a more focused, confident, and detached individual.

Three years into this new program, I was led to the Ascended Masters website.

I recall being in India and knowing that I was attending a class during my sleep time. The class was with a Master of the blue ray. I didn't know what a blue ray was, but I was plagued with thoughts of the ray and had to know what it represented. So I went to an Internet cafe in India and searched "blue ray." The search took me to the Ascended Masters website. I read the material about the blue ray and understood more about the energy that I was working with. As the months progressed, I continued reading more. I decided that I wanted to visit the portal described on the website. I contacted Verna and requested a visit.

These were the early days of the portal, and Verna assumed that I lived in New Zealand or Australia. I was the first United States citizen to visit the portal in New Zealand, and it was a short three-day visit. I immediately recognized Verna from a past life when I saw her; we had been close in our past lives. When I initially arrived, I was given the opportunity to get a measurement reading. This was a new concept for me, and I was curious to know my level of spiritual Ascension, given my spiritual program with Amma. I had the reading done when I arrived, and then again three days after I left, to assess my growth after having visited the portal. I learned at that time that I was at the Ascension level of a group of five, including Verna.

At the time, I didn't understand Verna's language about initiations, but my experience at the portal brought me to my knees. Each day, I practically crawled when I arrived, as the overhaul that I had experienced from the previous day was intense. I left New Zealand and maintained my communication with Verna while continuing my spiritual program with Amma. I now understand that I needed to complete my program with Amma before I could fully transition to this next program with the Ascended Masters.

A year later, I passed the fifth initiation, which released me from the cycle of rebirth due to clearing my karma and being at one hundred percent radiance and vibrancy. And four months before I passed the sixth initiation, I graduated from Amma's spiritual program. It was a bittersweet graduation because I was leaving the magical world of Amma. As usual, I did not know what was ahead of me. On one level, I was ready to leave her program and begin my next step; however, I would miss what was familiar. I would miss my world with Amma. But I knew that Amma had provided me with a solid mastery of spiritual concepts that I would later revisit as I worked towards higher initiations.

In truth, all spiritual programs are overseen by the hierarchy of Ascended Masters. Various people resonate with different spiritual programs. As our planet has evolved in consciousness, so has our opportunity to ascend, to complete higher levels of initiation. Levels that once required more effort to ascend to are now more easily accessible, without the use of past harsh methods that involved isolation and complete release from one's previous life. What has also changed is that the outward guru has been replaced by the inner guru. The common language of today is to find a guide in human form who can lead us to learn how to find our own inner guidance. The outer guide is just the starting point.

At the time of this writing, it has been slightly less than three years since I passed the seventh initiation, and I will be mid-way towards passing the eighth initiation in 2019, hopefully earlier in the year than later. I continue to ascend with all but one of the original five that I was grouped with when I first met Verna.

More than five years have passed since I left Amma's spiritual program. I have since introduced my husband and children to the Ascended Masters program in New Zealand, initially to support better mental and spiritual health, but now to watch with pride as they complete initiation after initiation. I turned to the Ascended Masters program in New Zealand to help heal, protect, and support my family as they have found their own unique way to ascend closer to the God within.

What makes this program unique is that there is a way to measure spiritual growth in a quantitative manner. Trusting the measurement has been supported with my personal observation of my growth and my family's growth. What is meant by growth? We are healthier. We are wiser. We are more balanced. We are making better decisions that are leading towards a less chaotic life. Each year, we know that we will be better people than we were the year before. I have seen miracles unfold as each member ascends. Deep-rooted angry relationships have been healed. Disabilities have been conquered, and healthier choices have been made. I wish every human being on our planet could begin this process of modern Ascension. The opportunity for meaningful growth is available to all. This is an exciting time in our planet's history.

After a series of significant stages, my Ascension path has led me to this current stage. I call this stage Being of Service. At the time of this writing, my current work is multi-fold in nature. For one, I have returned to working with special needs elementary school children; my heart expands when I work with these young children. I am also a source of support for fellow initiates that are actively ascending. And the energy work that was a big part of my earlier training is now being used to actively support groups of people around the world who are being persecuted by a dominating force, of various nationalities, genders, and social groups. My other energy work passion supports children around the world. My desire is to empower our next generation.

Ascension is not always easy. In order to grow, we must face our demons within. Modern Ascension has given me specific tools that help me efficiently face my inner and outer challenges. Modern Ascension is practical in nature. When one grows, one has more energy, more responsibility, and is of more service to mankind. We eventually get to a point in our Ascension process when the journey stops being about us, and becomes, instead, a journey about supporting others. My journey has refined me to become an instrument of change.

My journey, like your journey, will follow different stages. It is my hope that you will join me as we become one light that transforms our planet.

Blessings.

January, 2019

Chapter Ten

Tammy Manzo

My Ascension Lifetime

Life on the Third Ray of Unconditional Love is....
"A Total Eclipse of the Heart"

Song title by Jim Steinman

Looking back on it now, there may have been some clues in my younger days that this would be the lifetime of Ascension for me.

I was raised in a strict Catholic family. My grandparents lived only a block away from our church, and my grandmother sang in the choir every day. I went to Catholic school, and the entire school went to Mass every day. Back in the 1970s, there were still teachers who were nuns, and there was a time in which I wanted to be one too. I would find out from a past life reading from Verna and Waireti at the Ascended Masters Alpha Imaging website that I have had 2,016 religious past lives, as a priest, monk, nun, and so on. This had to be the lifetime for completion of some kind. But I would be forty-four years old before I would be able to break away from all this religious training and these memories.

I did love my church, Nativity of the Blessed Virgin Mary, which I still consider to be the most beautiful in the world. I loved the solemn, calming, and healing energy that was always present in this church. Back in the 70's, they still used incense and rang the bells every day during Mass, with candles lit everywhere. I could sit all day in this energy if they let me.

When I was in the second grade—that's the big year for the first sacraments of confession and communion—memories started bubbling up from my subconscious. I wouldn't know what was happening until I was an adult, but I started remembering past lives at that time—more specifically, the *trauma* of past lives. I developed fears, of the dark, of basements, of falling asleep with my back to the door of my room. I didn't tell anyone about what was happening. I just learned to deal with the fear, the panic, and the anxiety. There were feelings of shame, anger, and guilt that were deeply entrenched in me, that I didn't know the origin of. I prayed a lot at night in those younger years, and asked the angels to come around me and protect me; only once I felt their energy around me could I become calm and be able to sleep.

I didn't know too much about love. My family was not the touchy-feely type, and that included extended family on both sides. We didn't talk about love, or any other kind of emotions. Instead, my family showed its love in practical ways, by doing things for each other. We weren't exactly dysfunctional, but we weren't exactly nurturing. I would realize later in life that I was here to learn how to love and nurture myself. In the meantime, there was an inner struggle going on. My entire journey would be an inner one.

I didn't love myself. Because of the wild emotions and memories that wouldn't go away, I thought I was some kind of freak show. I spent a lot of energy trying to cover that up. I hid behind thick glasses and even thicker makeup, hoping that nobody would see what was inside me.

And so it wasn't easy for me to make friends or to be confident in any way. I thought there was something wrong with me, the way I was scared of so many things. I always just wanted to be like everybody else, what I considered "normal." I pretty much hated my life and everything in it. I couldn't wait until I could get out of school and move away, as far as I could. I blamed everything on my parents and their strict religiousness, which I began to rebel against. Somewhere I had heard the term "holy roller" and that summed it all up. I didn't want to be a holy roller any more.

The rebellion came out in a big way. I felt like I was fighting for my life, and I had to break away from everything that I had ever been told to believe or to think. I found astrology and studied that in my room, burning incense. The emotions were too much to bear, and I alternated between crying and screaming and yelling. I was so angry all the time. It was like a big wave that picked me up and carried me along, and I just tried to keep my head above water.

How my parents survived all of this is a mystery. I covered up a lot of it, and the rest probably passed for teenage angst. I didn't ask for help. I'm not sure if they ever knew what was going on. I'm not even sure what was going on myself, even all these years later.

But that wave of emotions started to subside as I got older. By the time I went to a small private college, there had been a big shift in my energy. I felt like I could finally create a new life, my own life, the one that I had wanted to have for years. I was determined to change everything about myself that I didn't like. I was going to have confidence in myself, start talking to people, and make myself do those things that I had been too scared to do before. I had to force myself at first, but it got easier as I went along.

My biggest achievement at college was walking up and down the dorms, knocking on doors, and introducing myself to the girls—and to some guys. For some kids, the biggest problem was being homesick or lonely or overwhelmed by the workload. For me, every day was a series of little things that I was afraid to do, that I eventually learned to do.

I joined a sorority and it really helped me learn to connect with others. It was like having an instant family of forty girls that were sharing their emotions all the time. They were always hugging me and each other. At first I felt silly and wondered why I was there. But the seed had been planted and was constantly being watered. It sprouted and grew, and there it was. It helped me to start feeling comfortable around love and to start seeing value in myself, even if it was through somebody else's eyes. But I still had really strong emotions rolling around inside me. I was fearful of being discovered as a fraud, that others would find out that I was really afraid of everything. And I still wouldn't sleep with my back to the door.

I graduated from college in the late 80's with a marketing degree. The next twelve years would be a huge cycle of personal growth for me. I got a job at a local newspaper in the outside retail advertising department. That meant I was going to have to leave the office and call on store owners to get them to buy ads in the newspaper. Me? Trying to get up the confidence to talk to professional business people? How was that going to work? It was one thing talking to kids on campus—but now I truly felt out of my league.

At first, I was so scared and shy that I was almost in tears. And there were times when I actually was in tears. Mother Mary must have really carried me then. Little by little, I had some success, and my confidence grew. And along the way I had gotten married, and it was about time to start a family.

I needed a less stressful job, and so I found one with the local library system. Each one of us was expected to read books at home as part of the job—well, you didn't have to ask me twice to do that! I loved to read, and it had always been an escape route for me. Every night I would leave the library with a canvas tote bag full of books, magazines, and movies. I absolutely loved that job. The extra bonus was that, as soon as I had started there, I found out I was pregnant.

My son was about two years old when my husband was offered a job that was too good to pass up. But it was going to conflict with the library and the daycare, so I gave up the easy job that I loved and took on the hardest job ever—I became a stay-at-home mom. This part of my life was when I really learned about unconditional love. Being with a toddler was all emotions, all the time, and I couldn't hide behind a briefcase anymore. I learned a lot about myself through this time with my son. I was determined to raise him differently than I had been raised. I hugged him and told him I loved him all the time. We talked about feelings, how we felt, and how to relate to others.

My soul had had a huge growth spurt, and I was starting to feel it. By 10:00 am each day, we had played with everything: Legos, Playdoh, crayons, paints, sandbox toys. It was something I had always wanted, and yet the feeling that something was missing had started to creep in. There was a very real sensation of waiting. I knew something was coming, but what? There was a Purpose coming; that was all that I knew.

I felt like there were more shifts and changes coming, and I was in a hurry to get things moving. It felt like it was something big, and I felt guilty for just coasting along. I was supposed to be doing something, but I didn't know what it was.

Soon my son grew old enough to attend to kindergarten at a community school, and they needed volunteers for everything. I was there a couple of times a week, helping in the school office, library, or with the classroom teacher. This felt like the Purpose that was coming, and I began to seriously think about becoming a teacher.

Then my son became afraid to go upstairs to his bedroom by himself. Soon he became afraid to go to sleep at night. He wanted to sleep with the lights on and music playing. This brought up all the memories of the old fears that I used to have as a child. We took him to a psychiatrist for a couple of sessions, but it seemed to make matters worse. Her idea was to reward my son with stickers every time he went upstairs by himself, and after a certain number of stickers, he would receive a toy. But my son just didn't care about the toys or stickers. The fear was real, and I knew what that fear felt like.

So I ditched the psychiatrist and did what I should have done in the first place—just talked to my son. He told me he was seeing shadowy gray shapes in his room and was hearing voices. This was something I didn't know too much about; I had read astrology and had had my tarot cards read many times before, but ghosts and spirits were things I hadn't given much thought to, things that happened to other people. Back in my library days, the psychic Sylvia Browne was very popular and I had started to read her books. They challenged the beliefs I had about religion, Heaven, God, and so many other things. I was afraid that if I kept reading them, I was going to end up leaving the church, so I stopped reading. I wasn't ready yet to "wake up".

But I was literally being knocked awake now. What my son was going through started the whole process of what seemed like the "fast track" to spiritual awakening. There was a book about psychic children by Sylvia Browne, so I started with that. Back then, there weren't a lot of other books about children that were like my son, the "crystal children," the ones that came in with their spiritual gifts intact.

Soon my son was seeing the shadowy figures with more clarity, and his guides started talking to him all the time, even waking him up in the middle of the night. I was excited to hear that Anubis was one of his main guides, because I loved ancient Egypt. My son would soon be able to read my past lives. He could see and exist on other dimensions at the same time. My son hated gym class, so Metatron would come to school and help him run laps. I had never even heard of Metatron. I was way out of my league again.

I had to get myself to the point where he could tell me anything and everything, so that meant letting go of everything I had ever believed before, from this life and every other past life. I was reading a lot of books then, and one that had had an especially poignant impact on me was *Many Lives, Many Masters* by Brian L. Weiss. It dealt with past lives and their memories, and it really resonated with me. This is when I started to realize that my early childhood memories were past life memories.

We had to go underground with all this information. Nobody around us was awake, and we kept all of what we were going through to ourselves. I even had to battle my husband at first with all of this. He wasn't overly religious, but the spirituality part was new to him and something he wasn't interested in exploring. He was happy to let me and my son believe in our stuff—he wasn't with us, but he wasn't against us.

My son also learned that he couldn't be open with any of his friends about who he really was and what his life was like. But people around him could sense that he was different anyway. He was bullied, even by his Boy Scout troop. He was a lonely child, and his journey could be a book in itself. I was always in awe of the spiritual wisdom that he had so naturally, and I struggled to keep up. He was never afraid, but I was.

Three years after my first little awakening, I still had one foot in the church and one foot out. My son was in third grade and he was still in our church's religion class. My plan was that once my son had all the sacraments, we would drop out completely. We only had a few more years to go until Confirmation. But he said to me that ninety percent of what they were teaching him in religion class was incorrect and he didn't want to go any more. My brain just about exploded.

It was one thing to rebel against religion when I was younger, because I could blame everything on my parents. But now this departure was going to be all on me—I was going to leave my religion as a deliberate, rational act. Or was I? I already felt that a lot of things about my religion didn't make sense to me, and there were holes in the belief system. I already knew, but I didn't want to know. But I knew my son, and I trusted his knowledge. I knew this was something we had to do. No more one foot in and one foot out.

I was giving myself permission to pursue the new knowledge of what my son knew, and of what I was learning about with each new spiritual book I read. I still loved things about the church—its incredible peaceful energy, Mother Mary—but I would keep those things while letting go of the rest that didn't fit with what I was learning. It was an extremely difficult process; all 2,016 of my religious past lives were in an uproar. So many old programs and beliefs and cellular memories had to be shifted; it really did feel like my brain had exploded. But everything had to go if I was to successfully birth yet another version of me.

I had created a space for new knowledge to come in, and it all came in quickly—reiki, tarot, numerology, palmistry, the spiritual laws of the universe, a deeper understanding of astrology, etc. Anything and everything related to energy and vibration, I was fascinated with. I started to hang out at the local metaphysical shop, taking classes and always learning something new—crystals, pendulums, how to sage a room, and so on. I was on a quest, and I was learning everything and anything I could get my hands on.

It was at the metaphysical shop that I met a healer who I would find out was a very close past life connection for me. At the time I just knew she was a psychic medium and healer. The healings she did started out as reiki sessions, but some years ago, the angels had come in during the sessions and created a new kind of healing. They released cords and blockages from past lives and then filled those spaces with beautiful, high vibration energy. I booked my session with her right away.

This was two years after I broke away from the church. I was a reiki master and teacher, but I worked mostly with family and friends. I did some work on myself but wasn't very consistent. I was still in the searching phase, both in my life and on my spiritual path. I still hadn't yet found the Purpose, but I felt it was getting close.

During an angelic healing session, my friend was shown by the angels something from one of my past lives that they wanted me to know. While the angels were removing it, she was describing it to me just like she was seeing a movie. It was France, 1700s, an arranged marriage. We were affluent, but there was a problem: I was not in love with my husband, but had fallen in love with somebody else. My husband found out, and one night while I was in bed, he stabbed me in the back five times with his sword.

After the angels removed that, I felt like I was a totally different person. This was the memory that I had carried around not only for forty years, but for many other lifetimes. I was so relieved to know that I wasn't crazy—it was real, and I hadn't been making it up. I felt physically lighter and, maybe for the first time in my life, happy. Thank you, angels!

I can now sleep anywhere with my back to the door. I can get up in the middle of the night and walk around without being terrified that somebody will come up behind me in the dark. The impending sense of dread that always used to be with me at night was gone.

I was also told that the person who had stabbed me in that lifetime was with me now in this lifetime, and that, together, we were working on forgiveness.

Shortly after this, more shifts happened. I started reading tarot cards at the metaphysical shop every month, at their psychic fair. At one of these fairs, one of my regular clients told me about St. Germain and the Ascended Masters. This saint was not one of the Catholic saints, and the Ascended Masters were not part of the Catholic religion. So I googled the Ascended Masters when I got home.

I found the Alpha Imaging website of the Ascended Masters portal in New Zealand right away. This was 2012, and was when my life really started changing. I signed up for the free Masters healing that they offered at that time—in fact, I signed up two different times for that healing. I found out Mother Mary was my Ascension teacher, and that meant so much to me. Of course she was, and had always been!

Over the next three years, I worked on myself consistently and with focus. I found other healers to work on me as well. I did not feel that sense of urgency, that wanting to get off the planet and never come back again, that others have felt. I had never thought about pursuing Ascension for myself. That was something that seemed far off, improbable and impossible. That was for Mother Mary and Jesus and all the other Masters. It almost seemed scary to think about it. I don't know if it was a lack of confidence or a sense of unworthiness, or whether it was the effect of more program or belief system from past lives, or all of the above—but back then, I wasn't thinking about Ascension.

My friend and I did many angel healings together over the years, and soon the angels didn't come anymore—Jesus and Mother Mary or Mary Magdalene came instead to heal us. I was going to a chiropractor every month for energy healing, spinal adjustments, and nutritional supplements. I was doing work on myself as well. I also found gifted healers from around the world through telesummits on the Internet.

As I continued moving along on my spiritual journey, many past life connections started to appear in my life. Some were to help me along, some I was to help along, and some were for karmic lessons. I was studying more and more about energy, astrology, the Akashic records, palmistry, crystals, essential oils, handwriting analysis, karma, past lives—anything considered New Age, I read about it.

There was a monthly astrology study group that I joined at the metaphysical shop that included many older spiritual people. Just to hear them talk each month blew my mind. It was there that I heard about shamans, Sufis, and other things that just don't show up in ordinary conversations. I was a sponge and absorbed everything. With this group I was blessed to experience winter solstice celebrations, despacho ceremonies, water blessing ceremonies, and even a Maypole ceremony. And there was a monthly reiki share at this shop that I participated in, each month for many years.

But still, with all these wonderfully wise people around me, nobody was actively working on Ascension, and it was never even brought up as a topic of discussion—and we talked about anything and everything else.

Soon I was working out of two shops, plus my home. I was still studying and doing the healings for myself and for others. And it was around this time that the idea of Ascension suddenly lit up for me. I don't know what brought it on. It had been building very slowly. This was the Purpose that I had felt was coming. It had been coming on all this time, like a gentle sunrise, and then there it was. It had taken me a while to get to this point, but I thought of all the healing I had done, and maybe it was time to see the fruit of my efforts.

I had my first chakra reading from Verna in June 2015, and it wasn't what I expected. I wasn't even at the third initiation. Two of my chakras were only at fifty percent vibrancy, although two were at seventy percent and the others were at sixty percent.

I was utterly astounded and totally crestfallen that there was still so much work to do, after I had done so much for so many years to change my entire life. Working with a measurable goal was what I was always used to, so I got focused and got moving quickly. The protection grid came first, then the oils and the Ascended Master healings. I had an updated reading six months later: I had lost six dimensional lives and had passed the third initiation. I had three chakras at seventy percent and four at sixty percent, and my heart chakra was turning pink. At the next reading in November 2016, I had lost three more dimensional lives. Three chakras were at eighty percent and three were at seventy percent. Time to get more oils and more Ascended Master healings. This was the reading in which Verna first suggested meditation as an Ascension tool, and in particular, the Torus technique. I wish I would have done the Torus at this point, but I didn't until later in my journey.

Six months later at the next reading on June 2017, six chakras were at eighty percent. One was holding me back. I only had six dimensional lives left, and my heart chakra had turned completely pink. Time for more oils, more healing. It was getting close now to the fourth initiation and I was afraid to be disappointed, so I held off on the next reading to do more concentrated work on myself.

In January 2018, I was surprised when Verna emailed me out of the blue—she had been filing some emails and noticed that I was past due for a sixth month checkup; did I want a reading? Yes please! Four chakras were at ninety percent and three were at eighty percent, putting me at the fourth initiation. She invited me to join the Facebook support group. I went to the Facebook group page about an hour later, and there were already many welcoming and congratulatory messages for me from the members.

I knew I was going to learn some really great information in that group, but here's what I had learned about my journey up until then: the healings that I and others were doing were not removing the karma from the chakras. If they were, it was at an extremely slow pace.

However, the healings did have value for me in that they helped release old emotions, cellular memory, and even old past life trauma. I became more peaceful, balanced, and calm. I did not have that constant hum of anxiety running in the background. The things that I had been afraid of as a child had been released. I was happy and healthy, and life was really good. But I had been ascending very slowly, until I started making Ascension my priority.

It wasn't until I started doing the Torus meditation regularly that things really started to shift quickly. As I got closer to the fifth initiation, the lower self (ego) must have figured out what was going to happen soon. It still wanted to hang on, so it brought out my old Achilles heel: fear. What I would call my "dark night of the soul" lasted a few months, in varying amounts of intensity. Before it was over, I came to understand that fear was only created in the mind, and it could be uncreated there as well. I had to lose faith in everything I thought I knew so that a complete transformation could come about.

About seven months after joining the group, on October 3, I received the email that I had passed the fifth initiation. On October 11, I received the email that the sixth initiation was beginning, and about a month later on November 13, was told the sixth initiation was complete. I could feel all the energetic shifts and changes happening through my body during this time. I would usually start to feel exhausted during the day; then, as I was falling asleep at night, the energy would start moving. It was never anything painful. Sometimes it would feel like pressure, the sensation of floating, or even like parts of the body being squeezed. I had always felt energy, so this was natural to me. I was grateful to feel these initiation ceremonies, and they helped me work even harder toward the next level.

I had never had the full ray reading, so all I know is that my Ascension ray is the third ray of Unconditional Love. Mother Mary is my Ascension teacher and Pallas Athena overlooks my dimensional lives. Higher Self is at twelve percent in body right now, and I've just learned that I have moved to the seventh ray, which is the violet ray, the Ray of Change, Transformation, and Transmutation—magic, the inner change and transformation versus external change. This is exactly what I've been doing all along. Now I can do it from within, willingly, without feeling pushed from outside forces. I work with my Higher Self every day to transform old patterns of thinking, believing, and behaving. Higher Self clears these things quickly and easily.

Around the fourth initiation, past life memories had started to surface regularly. I watched a lot of educational television and documentaries, and whenever a show featured a person or place in connection with a past life, I could feel the energy coming down through my crown. I would jot it down on a piece of paper and then take it to my Higher Self to clear. And travel shows are even more interesting, now that I can tell where I've lived before. With over 14,500 past lives, there aren't too many places that my soul hasn't been. It's really something to get a sense of the enormity of the soul and the Higher Self.

I can feel my Higher Self as he advances into the body. It feels like internal heat, usually radiating out from the heart space. Sometimes I feel this energy in the womb. There are times when I wake up in the morning and I feel this heat. I know this is my Higher Self and I feel like he has been working with me during the night. I love that feeling of togetherness. I've noticed that this usually happens after I do a group Torus with my family in the Ascended Masters Facebook group.

I can also tell when my Higher Self is with me during the day. When I am creating something artistic or crafty, I feel the energy pouring down into my crown and I feel pure joy and excitement in my heart. I don't spend a lot of time creating things with my hands, but at Christmas I love to make wreaths and other decorations. This past Christmas, Higher Self was with me when I was creating, and it was wonderful. It felt like we were truly one, like floating on air, something I've never felt before. It felt like true love.

I have also noticed Higher Self coming in when I do readings and healings. There is now sound vibration being channeled. There is more than one vibration/frequency, and I'm still learning and experimenting with this.

Now on the sixth initiation, I love this Earth even more, knowing that I may never come back here. I've never been in a hurry to quit this planet, but now I look at everything with new eyes, with gratitude and wonder. I am at peace with myself, and I'm happy to be here. I've learned how to love and accept myself, and because of that, I've learned to love and accept others as well. It's opened up an entirely new world for me. As an astrologer, I see a total eclipse as a portal for exponential growth. This journey has been a 'total eclipse of the heart' for me. It's a total transformation from where I started in this lifetime—and there is still more to come.

February, 2019

Chapter Eleven

Sheila Franzen

Unwavering Faith

"God grant me the serenity to accept the things I cannot change; courage to change the things I can; and wisdom to know the difference"

Reinhold Niebuhr

Ascension has always been in my awareness, from as young as I can remember. Growing up in a Lutheran household, I was in Sunday school from the time I was three or four years old. I have fond memories of learning all the Bible stories. Snapshots are still in my head of the pictures that show Elijah and Jesus ascending to the clouds in children's stories.

I was fascinated by this, and a part of me wondered how we could all do that. If someone before Jesus had done it, then that must mean that others could do it, too.

While I've always been fascinated by all things spiritual, New Age, and esoteric, my experience of life is quite grounded in this third dimension. My career has been in technology and management, with over twenty years of working in Corporate America. I'm not a healer or mystic or someone who can see energy or travel to other dimensions. I'm just an old soul that has known her entire life that it is time to move beyond physicality on earth to something more. I have learned trust and faith in something I can't see or hear, because I *know* that it's true.

Knowing seems to be one of my gifts. For me, it's very subtle, and I'm not always able to tell whether this knowing is originating from myself or whether it's coming from another source. I've longed to be able to tell the difference or to sense the wavelength of the thought, but this physical body I'm in doesn't seem to allow for that differentiation. The journey I share below is filled with moments of knowing.

The Early Years

My youth was spent growing up in a farming community in rural Illinois. While I didn't live on a farm, I grew up with the freedom that existed in small towns half a century ago. While I didn't necessarily love growing up in a small conservative town, I do appreciate the exploration and responsibility that I learned in the process.

My elementary school years from third through eighth grade were spent in a three-room country schoolhouse. Nope, it wasn't in 1920—it was in 1980. This was also where I began to question religion and its stories compared to science lessons. I wanted to know how they all fit together. I can still remember sitting in the basement of the schoolhouse during science class, asking the science teacher how God really created the world in seven days. It just wasn't possible in my mind. At some point, I knew the teacher was tired of my questions and so I stopped asking them. But, while I stopped asking them, they never stopped in my mind. I have been asking questions and trying to figure out and understand how this planet operates forever.

During those years of riding the bus to and from the little country school, I recall standing on the bus one day, holding my hands on both seats and thinking to myself, *there has to be more than this.* Life just felt so empty; it wasn't full. This passing thought didn't last long, but it was distinct. I have thought about this moment often, and I realize now that it was this moment that spurred me to try and find out more, to figure out more, to know more.

High School

Up through High School, I was actively involved in our church and youth group. I loved Sunday school, summer Bible school, the youth group, and the ritual of it all. In high school, we even explored the other churches in town, and I thought it was really neat to learn about the other religions and the differences that each proclaimed.

It wasn't until college that I felt like religion had betrayed me. I attended a small Methodist college, and we were required to take religion class. In that class, we learned that there are actually two stories of creation in the Bible. I found myself angry, as I had spent over twelve years learning in my church and no one had ever mentioned that there were two.

During this same time, I was also exploring my own identity around being lesbian. While visiting home and reluctantly attending church again, the pastor spoke about how homosexuality was wrong. I left church that day and didn't return until I was in my early thirties.

My experience of high school was good—on the surface. I was the all-star athlete, valedictorian of my high school class (albeit only 65 students), in all the clubs, Senior Class President, and an all-around nice person. Sounds pretty good, right? But no—I was miserable, alone, scared, and spent a good chunk of my time thinking about suicide and wondering how I could end it all. Life felt overwhelmingly painful and lonely, and I told no one—not my parents, friends, teachers, coaches, no one—about how I was actually feeling. I never attempted suicide, yet the thought was with me often back then, and it continues to plague me my entire adult life.

The Twenties and Thirties

After college, a close friend introduced me to Jane Robert's *Seth Material*. I was enamored by the concept that someone was sharing information from someone not on the planet. After all, my only introduction to aliens at that point had been *E.T.* My insatiable desire to understand was now ignited, and so began my relentless seeking.

At the age of twenty-seven, I moved to Portland, Oregon, from Atlanta, Georgia. The spiritual and alternative nature of Portland changed my life. I discovered a small spiritual community that focused on the celebration of life. We met weekly, and the services consisted of meditation, chanting, and an inspirational message. The messages were from a variety of religious backgrounds, peaking my interest in the exploration of different philosophies.

During these years of intense self-development, I attended seminars and workshops and meditation retreats. I spent hours and hours in bookstores, reading and learning. I was determined to find a reason for the fact that I didn't feel great about myself. I wanted to understand why joy seemed to elude me, why I was so critical of the world, and how I could find more peace.

My late twenties was also when I began meditating. I still remember the first time I attended a meditation class in a small New Age bookstore in Portland. We started with the concept of quieting one's mind. I remember almost laughing because I didn't think it was possible—and actually, I still don't find this easy. Sitting for three minutes felt like complete torture. *What was I supposed to do? How do you quiet your mind? How am I supposed to breathe? What? Where?*

Seriously? I loved it, and yet was completely perplexed by it. So I read books about it, I attended classes, and I got up every morning and meditated. The books said I would find peace and joy in meditation, so I did it. I wanted that more than anything. I desperately wanted to feel better.

Did it help? Sure. Did I ever find peace? Well, not really. My experience of meditation today is not much different from when I first started. It's a time for me to stop, breathe, and calm down. I'm a driven person, and once I decide to do something, I pursue it until I feel like I have mastered it. Yet meditation is still not something I feel I've mastered. I long to have the blissed-out journeys to other dimensions that I've read about in so many books. Yet to this day, for me, meditation is still an experience of darkness. I shut my eyes, and it's just black. There aren't colours, I don't see light or Angels or Masters or other dimensions. I don't hear anything and I don't physically sense anything. It's just peaceful, simple, and empty.

But maybe it's in the stillness of darkness that one can come to discover one's deepest self.

Never Again

I've had this deep, painful conviction since I started spiritual work in my twenties that I never wanted to have to live another life on this god-forsaken planet again. I have said many times, "We come here, we live, we die, and we kill each other." It boggles my mind that we are here in 2018 and still fighting over who and what God is. We humans are so stuck in our cycles of karma that we can't see out. This feeling of never wanting to live on this planet again was my motivation to continue spiritual seeking until I found the answers I was looking for, a hopeful response to the statement that had hung in my mind since I was ten years old: *There has to be more to life than this.*

This thought carried within it the seed that blossomed into my journey, my journey to Ascension and freedom from the cycles of incarnation.

Jeshua

I grew up with Jesus as my teacher. After all, that is what Christianity is. Yet we were taught to worship him. As an Ascended Master, Jesus (or Jeshua) has teachings on this planet that span far and wide. He has worked through many Souls and always mentions that they have agreements to bring forth the truth that is shared.

Whether his words are shared in books like *A Course in Miracles* or *The Way of Mastery* or *Love Without End*, the message is always the same. The message is about love. He shares similar stories in all of his teachings; while he was on this planet, his message was about love—not worship—and he's still teaching it to us today. There are many individuals who channel his words today. This Being's commitment to Earth and its evolution is beyond words. He walks with many.

One of my favourite stories of Jeshua working with people in today's world is Glenda Green's portrait of Jeshua. She was asked to paint a portrait and refused to because she couldn't see him. Then he appeared to her and opened her third eye, and sat with her for months while she painted his portrait. Her journey with him is chronicled in *Love Without End*. The story is amazingly beautiful. I happened to read the book a second time while I was living in Texas and discovered that the original painting was in a small church with the Christ Truth League in Texas. That same week, I got in my car and drove to see the original painting. People from all over the world travel to see it each year. It is stunning. The brilliance of the colour and the energy of the painting are amazing. It feels like a portal for Jeshua's energy and love.

While *A Course in Miracles* (channeled by Helen Schucman) from Jeshua is profound, it just wasn't the right information for me in the right format. The teachings that did resonate from Jeshua that had the largest impact on my life were from *The Way of Mastery* teachings through the channel Jayem. I still reread the books periodically, and the exercises on forgiveness are some of the most powerful I've ever found. And then there is the more recent work that Mari Perron has channeled through Jesus called *A Course of Love*, which is the continuation of *A Course in Miracles*. Her words have a softer message and seem easier to absorb. Gentle words for tumultuous times. Sometimes the teachings seem so simple, yet they are extremely powerful.

My family and children often ask if I believe in Jesus. My response is that I believe that Jesus walked the Earth for us to learn how to love more, that he was a teacher that wanted us to live a life full of love for ourselves and for one another. But I don't believe that he died for us. He died because there were mean, terrible people on the planet that killed him. He died because that was part of his journey. He lives and teaches us today because that is part of his journey. He never wanted to be worshiped. I often sense that the great spiritual teachers wonder why we worship them. They were just humans in their process of Ascension that made it further than most do while on this planet. If our focus was to learn from them and not worship them, then we would all be ascending much faster.

What makes me stand in awe of this Being known as Jeshua is that he finds new people to share information through, decade after decade. He may have walked the earth two thousand years ago, yet he is still teaching and finding new ways to share the message of love in the universe. What a commitment from this Christ Light. So I honour him and thank him, but I don't worship him.

Angels

I've always loved the stories of the Angels in the Bible from my childhood. They have this feeling of being white beautiful Beings. I've read many books in which people share their experiences of the Angels. It simply fascinates me. I feel like I'm blind to what is really going on. A part of me hopes that, one day, I will have a different experience of this.

One of the more recent books about Angels that expanded my understanding and awareness of the importance of them in our lives is *Angels in My Hair* by Lorna Byrne. She has been seeing and conversing with angels since she was two years old. Her book describes growing up with the Angels and her journey through life with them. Angels are everywhere, helping us all the time. After reading this book, I find that I intentionally thank the Angels more often and share my gratitude for their work in the world. It's also been a wonderful book that my children love listening to as well.

Meeting the Masters

In my early thirties, I was referred to a set of books called *The Life and Teachings of the Masters of the Far East* by Baird T. Spalding. I read these books and devoured them. I don't recall details of them now, yet I knew they were true and I knew that there was a set of Ascended Masters supporting this planet.

Another book that someone had shared with me was the first book in the *I AM Discourses* by Godfrey Ray King. I distinctly remember the first time I read it. I was on a plane flying overseas. I finished the book and started it over from the beginning. The book is Godfrey Ray's journey with St Germain through a world on this planet that we don't see. This is a world of the energy of the Masters and Beings, who take care of, support, and work on this planet. The seed had been planted and the concept of I AM lodged into my awareness. I wanted to meet the Ascended Masters. I wanted to visit these places. I wanted conscious awareness of these places.

Around age forty-five, after settling into motherhood, I found myself returning to the *I AM Discourses*. I wanted to remember the beauty of St Germain's journey with Godfrey Ray King. So I started reading the books again. This time, I read up to book ten. In that time, I also started saying affirmations every day for at least twenty minutes. I ordered the original affirmation books from the *Discourses* and decided that if I was going to have an experience of moving past physical life, I had to do the work. So I returned to many of the spiritual teachings that I had previously read, determined to find a way to not return to earth. I wanted to ascend.

Discovering the Ascended Masters Portal - August 5th, 2016

A year after reading the *I AM Discourses* again, I started reading a book that someone had recommended to me called *E-Squared* by Pam Grout. The book describes a series of exercises designed to help one realize that one creates one's own reality, with the universe's support. Grout's humour brings a lightness to what is typically a serious subject.

Here are my journal entries from the first exercise.

> *Friday, August 5th, 10:41pm*
>
> *Asked for a blessing and to be shown the blessing.*
>
> *Saturday, August 6th, 9:26 pm*
>
> *I thought about the blessing I had requested many times today and asked to be reminded of receiving it.*
>
> *I was guided to search for Ascended Master healing tonight and found a site in New Zealand where they offer free healings. The energy is so pure. I sent an*

> *email and asked to be healed through the portal. I am grateful for my blessing. I have found what I need! And I am guiding the universe!*
>
> *Oh, and less than 24 hours!*

My life had changed. I had found home.

Within a week, I had read everything on the portal site at alphaimaging.co.nz. While that probably doesn't sound like much, the blog contained weekly entries since 2010—there was a *lot* to read. I printed the blessing stone and put a pitcher of water on to drink every night. I'm still doing this, two years later.

Within eleven days, I had ordered a shawl and oils, received a chakra reading, and had a protection grid put in place. I was so grateful to have finally found the tools that could help me ascend that I could not get enough fast enough. I remember having a fear that these items would get lost or would stop working and that I'd have to come back to Earth again. From the day I received them, the oils have been a part of my daily routine. I meditate with a shawl every day, and often work with one wrapped around me. I sleep with one under my sheets and travel with them as well.

My Rays

As part of the Ascension process, one of the readings you can receive is a Five Ray reading where you learn the rays you have settled into for this incarnation. My rays were 1-2-3-4-5. This seemed a bit unusual to have five rays in sequential order. I guess things were aligning for me!

For each Ascension ray, a master also steps forward to assist you on that ray. These Masters were the team that has guided and supported me my entire life. I remember first reading this, and feeling so unbelievably humbled that I had a team of Masters willing to help me. The amazing thing is that they are here to help *everyone* on the planet.

Ascension Ray (Melchizidek) - 1st ray; blue, red, and silver ray of God's Will, Power, and Divinity

Life Ray (Jesus) – 2nd ray; the yellow ray of Wisdom, Joy, and Lightness of Being

Mental Body Ray (Kuan Yin) - 3rd ray; the pink ray of Unconditional Love

Emotional Body Ray (Serapis Bey) – 4th ray; the white ray of Harmony through Conflict

Physical Body Ray (Hilarion) - 5th ray; the green and orange ray of Healing, Knowledge, and Truth

My Ascension ray colour was blue. To be honest, this colour never resonated with me all that much. I haven't actually loved a deep blue this lifetime. I've always felt that wearing the colour makes me look pale, and everything I associate with deep blue doesn't necessarily resonate with me. Yet this was my Ascension ray colour. It is what it is.

Ascending on the first ray indicated that I would struggle with my power versus God's power. This part totally resonated with me, as I was aware that I've not been overly willing to trust in God or rely on religion. I've always had faith that there was a higher power, but because I can't fully understand it in this physical body, I've not always been very willing to turn my life over to it. I feel like my journey of Ascension was a continued journey of learning to trust the Masters and the God Within.

Melchizidek was my Ascension Master. The Five Ray reading that I had received shared the following:

> *As a first ray soul, your soul lessons will be around Power and Will—God's will over your will, and then your will over the will of others, and others' will over you. This then impacts on personal power. This power play of will is a major lesson for those with Melchizedek. These are very powerful lessons and ones that need to be learnt at a heart level, not a head level. Melchizedek works with the lesson of perseverance. Those with Melchizedek have in past lives been part of the Melchizedek order.*

I wanted to get to know Melchizidek. I wanted to know more about who he was and what he did while he journeyed on this earth. I wanted to know what he taught. I searched for books and read what I could find on the Internet. None of it really resonated with me. So I had to let all of that go and trust that when I sat and meditated and asked for his presence and his teachings, I would learn what I needed to know.

I know that he stood with me and supported me and guided me, and at the same time, I must admit that he always felt distant to me. Yet, looking back, I realize that this is how I held my view of him. In my journey through Ascension and working with Melchizidek, I came to realize that I felt like I had let him down in many other lifetimes because I had followed his work and not yet ascended. I realized that I felt like a failure because I had been a student and here I was, who knows how many lives later, still trying to ascend. I realized that I was afraid to trust again because I didn't want to fail. I had to work through my feelings and beliefs and frustrations with failure in order to forgive and let go, and let go and forgive. I used the Deva of Forgiveness oil on a regular basis as I journeyed through learning to love myself and the Masters.

Initiations

When I started working with the Masters through the portal, I had already passed the third initiation. The ability to have some idea of where I was on my journey through the initiations was such a gift. About six months later, I passed the fourth initiation on my birthday in February of 2017.

Reading through my journal during this time, I'm reminded of the amount of work I did surrounding trust, acceptance, and forgiveness. Working through the challenges of power as a first-ray dominated my journey. While I spent a great deal of time working out my issues of power with God, I spent even more time working out the issue of power with my children. I came to the realization that the gift that one of my daughters was providing me with was the opportunity to surrender. While it didn't necessarily feel like a gift, as I look back, I fully understand the soul support that we are providing each other. My relationship with my daughters is also where I worked through my fourth ray growth for my emotional body of harmony through conflict.

With the second ray of Wisdom, Joy, and Lightness of Being, Jesus continued to work with me. Honestly, I'm not sure I still fully get it. My purpose and passion around Ascension has kept me serious and focused. I like to be busy and I like to accomplish things. I have to schedule free time in my life so that I allow fun and joy to find its place.

For the third ray of Unconditional Love (mental body) with Kuan Yin, I requested a crystal portal. I think that unconditional love is where my journey of acceptance showed up. I meditated with the portal often and used her oil for Inner Peace every night before bed. I practiced looking at everyone and everything in my life to understand where I stood in judgment over acceptance. Finding acceptance allowed me step into more love.

During my journey from the fourth to the fifth initiation, I spent a significant portion of my daily hours with my mother in her last year of life here on earth. While our relationship had never been one of depth, I know that her allowance of my love and care was part of my learning in unconditional love. In one of those rare moments in which a visualization worked for me in my meditations, she appeared to me, and I knew that our time together had been part of my Ascension path. Thank you, Mom.

The fifth ray, the green and orange ray of Healing, Knowledge, and Truth (physical body) with Hilarion was challenged during this time of Ascension. I injured my right knee not long after the fourth initiation and was in continual pain, and this eventually led to a surgery six months later. I also injured my right shoulder during this time, which also required attention. I'm sure part of the injuries were due to clearing and healing on the path to Ascension.

Free from the Cycles of Rebirth – Passing the Fifth Initiation, May 14th, 2018

On May 14th, 2018, I received confirmation that I had passed the fifth initiation. The joy that I felt that day lasted about twenty-four hours. I did not want to go to bed that night because I didn't want the joy to go away. I had never experienced joy like this before. While Verna has a detailed description of each phase of Ascension on the website, I felt none of those things. I didn't know I had passed the fifth initiation until I received the email confirming it. I had felt a bit off that day, but I had no awareness in my meditation that morning or my experience that day that it had happened. Yet when I knew it was complete, I was overjoyed. The relief that I felt knowing that I would not have to return to earth again had me feeling as though I was floating off the ground.

When I awoke the next morning, I was still joyful, yet the intense joy from the previous day had settled. Over the next days, as the knowledge settled in that I was free from the cycles of life on earth, my perspective shifted. As life settled back into the day-to-day, there was also a sense of "now what?" The drive, the longing, the seeking—it was over. I had accomplished my mission to ascend and not return to earth.

Life after the Sixth Initiation—Getting to Know the Higher Self

My Higher Self is around thirty percent settled in my Holy Heart as I write this. My experiences of Higher Self are not distinct. I don't always know whether it's her, my mind, or some other Being sharing information with me. It is subtle. I would rather it be a screaming voice in my head—yet it's not. I've learned to trust a technique that I learned many years ago about feeling a sensation in my body around my heart. Again, this is so subtle that it's not always clear, yet I trust it because it's always right. I take a moment and breathe. Then I ask a question, and if I feel the energy or a sensation rise up in my chest, I know it's a *yes* and I should move forward with it. If the energy or the sensation drops down, then it's *no*. This awareness brings me back into my body and into my heart the best way that I know how to at this point.

While there is continual spiritual growth happening, there has also been a significant return to some physical needs. I've been one to search out healers for decades now. I don't particularly like the healthcare system. While they are fantastic at crisis management, they don't seem to solve long-term care issues at all. Besides, I want *healing*. I want things to change forever, not a bandage.

A year ago, I had knee surgery to remove part of a torn meniscus. The injury required a long process of healing. While I did many spiritual healings with others around my knee, seven months after the surgery, I was moving less than I was before the surgery. During a visit to my in-laws, I had this sense (Higher Self guiding me) that I needed to get a massage. This was a bit unusual, as I had never sought out a massage in the ten years that I've been visiting where they live. So when one of my partner's friends was over, I asked if she knew anyone that was good at massage, and she said she did. I scheduled the massage, and within fifteen minutes of being there, she said I should get the book *Pain Free* by Peter Egoscue. This book has turned out to be a major part of my physical transformation to lessen pain. I read the book and started doing the exercises immediately and found relief. I discovered a local clinic where I lived and have been going there regularly since then.

Sometimes our bodies need physical support. We can do all the spiritual healing we want, but if we aren't actually using the muscles that we have in these amazing bodies, they stop working. Before I started, I could not stand up from a chair without significant help from my arms, and I couldn't lift my shoulder above my head. After daily work, I walked five kilometers a month ago and feel stronger than I have in a long time. Plus, with a focus on postural alignment, I think I've grown an inch. I know that my Higher Self guided me to the right massage therapist to find this book.

The second way that she has guided me is around the food that I'm consuming. I have had my share of health problems over the years. As one doctor told me, "you must have incredible will power because the amount of inflammation you have would typically have someone in bed!" At almost fifty, it's been catching up with me.

Higher Self recently guided me to what she wanted me to know. I was scrolling Facebook one evening and an ad about celery juice came across my feed. I remember thinking, *seriously, not another fad*, and scrolling by it. But I kept feeling this nagging to go back and watch the video (Higher Self guiding me), so I did. I was intrigued more by the name of the Facebook page, Medical Medium. I went to the website and discovered that Anthony William, the website's creator, has been hearing a voice outside his right ear since he was four years old. This voice, Spirit of the Most High (Compassion), shares with him what is physically wrong with every person he meets or sees. I bought his book, *Liver Rescue,* and read the four-hundred-page book in several days.

With Spirit, he shares information that they say is twenty to thirty years in the future. The depth and precision with which he speaks about disease, illness, and root causes blew my mind. Thank you, Higher Self! I now understand my aches and pains and why I've been so miserable for so long. I've also had many revelations around my mother's health and what contributed to an early passing for her.

The biggest change for me has been the freedom to eat fruit again. He shares that the ideal fuel for the health and support of the liver and brain is the glucose from fruit. In two weeks of doing celery juice every morning and eating all the fruit I want, I feel amazing! Seriously, I haven't felt this good in twenty years. My head is clear, my meditations are deeper, I'm not tired, I'm more joyful, I'm losing weight, and I have the energy to be with those around me. I've even stopped medications I was taking and am relieved to know that I'm on a journey to a healthier body that will support me the rest of my life. Who knew that discovering a new depth of joy would actually be a physical need related to food in my body versus a spiritual healing? Thank you, Higher Self.

Reflections on Ascension

Everyone's relationship with Higher Self is their relationship with God. We often think of God as this external entity, yet in reality our God is our Higher Self and much closer to us than we realize. I've spent lifetimes trying to discover God and connect to God. This lifetime, I have spent my entire adult life in pursuit of this. Much of it has been in pursuit of finding the ultimate spiritual experience. Yet, as the days go by, I realize that it is in the small moments of laughter with my family or seeing beauty in an unexpected place that the experience of humanity resides.

While Ascension hasn't turned out to be floating away into the heavens, I am beyond grateful for my journey. I am so humbled for the years that Mother Earth and the Masters have spent supporting me and humanity.

Ascension is a journey of lifetimes and a journey of commitment. One does not ascend without intention. While we are all continuously on a journey of Ascension, we are not all actively ascending. Ascension requires action. It requires that you put in the work, the effort, and the commitment.

I often feel that my Ascension journey is rather unexciting. I can talk about the knowledge that I've learned from reading about others' experiences, yet my experience is pretty simple and uneventful. I have had to rely on my commitment to not return to this earth. I often feel that my journey of Ascension is kind of like being blindfolded with headphones on in the dark. I have learned to trust the subtle knowing that I sense. Yet at the same time, it's been one of blind faith and trust.

I do know I am destined to serve in a larger way. I have known this for as long as I can remember. I don't know how or what or when, but I know the day will come. For now, I serve in physical form by doing what I can for my family, my friends, and my clients. I am honoured to be a vehicle for my Higher Self and her expression. I can't wait to see what that expression turns into as she settles fully into this physical body.

December, 2018

Chapter Twelve

Andrew Logan

The Benevolent Universe

"Life is a Miracle in disguise. How blessed we are when the disguise is seen through, even temporarily".

Andrew Logan

Growing up, it seems I had a fairly normal childhood. I was very sensitive, and also quite shy, but overall things worked out for me without any major complications.

A memorable experience I had with a friend when we were around twelve years old occurred in the basement of my family's house. We were walking towards the stairs, having just turned off the lights, when we both happened to look backwards down the hall at the same time. There, floating a few feet above the floor, was a glowing radiant white orb of light that seemed intelligent. Once we saw it, it started to slowly float towards us, which of course scared us both into running upstairs. I feel now, in hindsight, that it was probably a benevolent spiritual being, but at the time I didn't really have too many concepts about that.

A second memorable experience happened around fourteen years old, when I was in my bedroom. I suddenly was absorbed into a trance-like state and heard an incomprehensible mystical-sounding language flow through my being. Now, in hindsight, I think this was probably a form of Light Language, offering a hint of things to come.

Other than a few spiritual experiences like these, though, my childhood was relatively normal.

As a teenager and into my years at university, I got into the habit of using marijuana, and after that, using some more powerful forms of psychedelic drugs like LSD, psilocybin mushrooms, ayahuasca, and mescaline cactus. These experiences were certainly mind-expanding at the time, making me question my cultural conditioning and inspiring me to work at peeling away layers of identity.

One particular experience after consuming psilocybin mushrooms stands out as particularly transformative. After consuming them, I started seeing and processing all the events and details of my life in rapid succession, while feeling like I was undergoing some sort of death. It was quite terrifying. After a while of this, I experienced what can be called ego-death—the temporary suspension of one's ego—and was submerged into a vast sea of blissful vibration for what felt like an eternity. When I came out of the experience the next morning, it felt like I had been reborn, and forever changed by the experience.

For me, these substances offered an entryway into spiritual experiences and spiritual interests, but by no means are they the best approach for most. I would say any experience that occurs on these psychedelic drugs can more safely be cultivated through meditation, and many people have misused these substances and suffered consequences. For me, though, they opened a door and sparked a deep interest in spirituality at the time.

Towards the end of university, I stumbled upon some spiritual books that proved to be quite influential in my life, most notably *Autobiography of a Yogi* by Paramhansa Yogananda. I remember reading most (if not all) of it in one long sitting, totally captivated by the stories it contained, and totally inspired to pursue my spiritual path in earnest. This led me to begin attending Buddhist teachings at a nearby Tibetan Buddhist center while on a co-op work-term for school. The first meditation we did, and my first "official" meditation session in this life, was Tonglen, which is the Tibetan Buddhist practice of inhaling the transformation of others' suffering and exhaling your happiness to them. As I was doing the meditation, I found myself suddenly transported in a vision as lucid as waking reality to a room with the Dalai Lama, who put some prayer beads around my neck. I took this experience as a sign of being welcomed into the Tibetan Buddhist tradition.

Around this same time, while at home contemplating the thought that everything is divine light, I suddenly fell onto my bed and was absorbed into an infinite sea of seemingly omniscient golden light. This remains the most profound experience of my life—I was at one with the infinite light, there was no center and no edge to it, no beginning, middle or end, without movement yet constantly expanding. It was a state of seemingly infinite bliss as well, what can be described as perfection; but there were no thoughts in this state—just a perfect knowing. When I came out of that state, I found that two hours had passed in earthly time, but it had felt like an eternity. I later heard about states of samadhi, and it matched the description of what I had experienced. This was a gift to me and, in some ways, a teaser to show what potential lies ahead. After coming out of this, I felt I had been healed and reborn on every level.

I quickly submerged myself in Tibetan Buddhism, and soon found a Buddhist guru and joined his ten-year at-home meditation program. It consisted of a minimum of two hours of daily meditation as we, as a group, progressed through a Tibetan Buddhist curriculum of meditation and practices. From my time with this program, I gained a great habit of daily meditation, discipline, and consistency. As well, I found that the Buddhist tradition inspired other great qualities, like the Bodhisattva ideal of universal altruism; the aspiration for perfect enlightenment; and the teachings on the Six Paramitas (perfections), which are generosity, moral discipline, patience, joyful effort, concentration, and wisdom. Overall, the tradition provided a framework for me to work on myself, and I see it as having been a great asset to my development and spiritual aspirations.

While in the meditation program, though, I encountered a very persistent and annoying obstacle: some form of spiritual entity obdurately distracted me in meditation and made things really difficult. This proved to be a very hard time for me, and I remember breaking down and crying during some meditations as it became so difficult. I was constantly torn between feelings of frustration with the two hours of daily meditation and of fear of falling behind and being forced to leave the program.

But, though hidden at the time, this episode with the entity was not without its blessings. As a result of struggling and not being able to resolve the issue through Buddhist practice alone (even after reciting a seven-line prayer one hundred thousand times, as per my guru's instruction), I was led to look for outside help in the form of spiritual healers. This was my entry into the world of spiritual healing, and I worked with a number of talented healers over many sessions and over a couple of years. One healer led to another, opening up my spiritual worldview beyond the Buddhist path, as well as providing my being with beneficial healing. What most of the healers agreed upon after some time was that this was not an external entity like I had thought, but rather was a part of my own being. After the whole ordeal ended, I was shown that it was my higher being skillfully guiding me down a new path in a very unconventional (and uncomfortable) way. On the plus side though, the experience was a great opportunity to cultivate greater patience and perseverance, two of the six Paramitas of Buddhism.

With my new expanded worldview of spirituality, I was eventually guided to leave the meditation program, much to my dismay. I was very sad to leave, as I had grown emotionally attached to the practices and the path it presented, but Spirit had a new path in mind for me. Around the same time, I stumbled across a spiritual practitioner who worked with the Ascended Masters and Angels and was starting a series of channeled courses that they had inspired. This was a time of much new learning for me, as I learned more about the Ascended Masters, the path of Ascension, the evolution they offered, the Angelic realms, the Christed Extraterrestrials (predominantly the Arcturian beings), and many other important spiritual concepts.

I was guided at this time (around 2013) to start a spiritual healing practice of my own, and had some good success with it. I used what I had learned from other healers and my own guidance, and had some good feedback from clients. After a short time, however, I was guided to stop offering healing, and was told I would resume it in the future. This had just been a sneak peek.

In search of more healing, and with my new appreciation of the Ascended Masters, I did some web searches for Ascended Masters healing and came across the Alpha Imaging site. I was instantly hooked on receiving the healing sessions and using the oils and other products. This was my new path, and I continued to receive sessions and work with all the oils. I learned from Verna that I was on the first ray as my Ascension ray, which is the ray of focus, balance, and God's Will over the Individual Will. I learned that my personality ray was the seventh ray, the ray of Change and Transformation. Put together, these two rays highlighted my focused and surrendered intent on personal and spiritual transformation. In some ways this combination contributed to a serious focus, but one for which I was glad, as I highly valued transformation in all ways.

After some time with this, I passed the fourth initiation and joined the online Ascension group, which became my new spiritual family. I remember how on the first day of joining, when I read all the welcoming messages from other members, I was flooded with a very strong wave of love.

I had a major life challenge towards the end of the fourth initiation, before passing the fifth initiation. There was a mole that had grown quite large, and turned out to be cancerous melanoma, the bad kind of skin cancer. It was a very scary time for me, as I had no idea how severe the cancer was or what would happen. I truly thought it might be fatal, or at least require a very long treatment and healing process. Thankfully it turned out to be early stage, and just required two surgeries to treat, and with a low chance of recurrence. I see this now as having been both a test, an opportunity for a lot of learning in a short time, as well as being a way of getting rid of the last bit of karma before passing the fifth initiation. As challenging as the experience had been, I see that I learned a great deal from it. It was not without its hidden value.

The path of spiritual development and Ascension is not without its many challenges, as all human lives seem to have. But I have come to see and believe that we live in a very benevolent universe, that Earth is a school, and that every seeming negative has a positive to it as well. Sometimes the lessons are very hard, but Spirit knows what it is doing to guide us to the learning, lessons, and life path that our souls seek. It can be hard to keep this in mind while in the midst of a major life challenge, but I have found it usually becomes more apparent in hindsight after things have settled and we are able to see the bigger picture.

Soon after passing the fifth initiation, I passed the sixth initiation and began meditating with my Higher Self, the Ascended Masters, Archangels, and Elohim more often, in the Torus sessions and private meditations. I found that my Higher Self's ray, and thus my new ray, was the second ray of Wisdom, Joy, and Lightness of Being. I find this new ray a real joy to be on, but of course, the path of mastery is not without challenges still. I am blessed to now have five crystal portals that I meditate with on a daily basis; these are crystals that have been made into portals for individual Masters, Archangels, and Elohim to work through. I am so grateful to have this level of support and continual training.

In 2017 I was guided to begin offering healing services again, this time with the assistance of my God Self (the higher self of my Higher Self). As well, my ability to channel Light Language activated for me, which provided another form of healing I could offer to others. Over time, these offerings have evolved a bit and expanded, and I have learned a great deal by being in the role of a spiritual facilitator.

At the beginning of 2019, I was blessed to pass the seventh initiation, completing the initiation during the lunar eclipse, which is supposed to be a time of completions and new beginnings, and thus was very fitting. Immediately after passing it, I felt a heightened sense of calm, balance, and acceptance. I feel that much is yet to come for me as I deepen into the seventh initiation and develop further. I look forward to the years ahead of service and learning, and am excited to see where the path leads from here.

I feel that everyone's spiritual path will be in many ways unique to them, though, of course, with some overlap as well. We are each called and guided down the path that is best for us; we just need to hold trust and faith, and keep our spiritual aspirations high.

January, 2019

Chapter Thirteen

Verna Maruata

My Perfect Path

"Be in your power; follow your own inner guru." -

Ares

Namaste.

My name is Verna Maruata. I am a guardian at the Ascended Masters' portal in New Zealand. I have passed the seventh initiation, and in the next year or so, I will pass the eighth initiation.

Ascension is the journey from the darkness into light. The darkness resides not in our minds, nor our bodies, but in our chakras. The darkness is our karma. We accrue karma daily with our thoughts, words, and actions. We ascend by paying our karma from this life and past lives. As our karma reduces, our light increases and consciousness rises.

Modern Ascension recognizes this base premise for Ascension. It cuts away religion, dogma, and ritual until all we have is the core. Ascension then becomes tangible and attainable.

This is my journey from my own karmic darkness into my light, and beyond.

I was born on the first ray for my Ascension, life, emotional, and physical bodies. This is the ray of God's Will and Power. The only relief from this masculine ray was that my mental body was on the third ray of Unconditional Love. My rays at birth read 1-1-3-1-1. El Morya was my Ascension Master, life ray master, and emotional body ray Master. Sitatapatra was my physical body ray Master, and Kuan Yin walked with me on my mental body ray. She, too, is a warrior, but on the third ray. So I was born a woman on the warrior ray, the ray of God's Will over Personal Will, the ray of personal power with the lessons of respecting the will of others and the use of power over myself and others. With El Morya, I had the aspect of focus. "If you want a job done, ask someone who has El Morya with them." And as my destiny played out, it came to pass that the Ascended Masters had a big job for me to do.

The first ray is not a friendly ray; those of us on the ray can be quite bossy. We lead, direct, demand, and expect everyone to keep up with us as we plan, teach, and create. Our manner can be abrupt, and that can be too much for most people. It is far easier to follow a first ray with El Morya than to walk beside them. My third ray mental body saved the day for me, for it meant I thought from the heart, not from my head. Compassion was part of who I was from a young age.

So back then, in the first stage of my Ascension, we see me as a bossy boot with heart.

I came from a long line of spiritual and psychic women of Scottish and Irish descent on both sides of my family. These were women who believed in healing energy, both from nature and from a higher power. We were born with gifts; our ancestors had gifts, and these gifts continue with my children and, I assume, my grandchildren. My gifts are healing, clairsentience, some foresight, and the ability to determine the darkness in people and, more specifically, soul eaters. Soul eaters are people who have no light and exude no energy.

My mother taught me to be authentic with my family. This meant knowing her beliefs and her gifts. In turn, I wanted my children to grow up with the authentic me, knowing my gifts and beliefs. It isn't always easy, especially as I change and ascend. My authentic self begins with my family and is supported by my ancestors.

I was told by family that I gave my first public healing when I was three. My parents woke at dawn to find me missing from the house. After a general neighbourhood panic, I was found at the bedside of a lady new to the street, who had come home from the hospital the day before. I was at her bedside when she woke every morning until she recovered.

Part of my heritage taught by my mother was to believe that reincarnation and past lives were a reality. This has always been an inner truth, supported by my own knowing and experiences. From the time I was a small child, I had a deep and abiding love for God. This was my own personal and private relationship that had nothing to do with religion. My mother was a religious woman and somehow managed to reconcile her religious beliefs with her personal truths.

I found Christianity much harder to accept; it never seemed to fit. We were taught we only had one life, and if we were good people, we would go to heaven. I knew this wasn't true. In fact, I knew in my core this wasn't true because I remembered my past lives. Why were we being told lies? If that wasn't true in the Bible, than what else wasn't true?

This was the first time I realized that my fact and someone else's fact were not the same. I became a non-believer in everything, and only decided something was true if it sat with my own inner knowing. Discernment in all things became my motto. I later learned that one of the early ecumenical councils removed all references to reincarnation from the Bible. If true, then by doing this, and thereby reducing Christianity to the belief of one life only, they had denied Christianity of one of the core truths of humanity.

In my teens, I became inclined towards the belief systems of Hinduism and Buddhism, as these reconciled with my personal beliefs and experience of reincarnation, God, karma, and Ascension. Beliefs for me never equated to religion. As a true first-ray, I preferred my own path, and I preferred my path to be clear and clean, not muddied by the dogma and ceremony of religion. I became very good at removing the unnecessary from my life.

I prayed and meditated daily, sometimes into a state of bliss. At one stage, I had a day of silence once a week. I had many beautiful and mystical experiences between just me and God—no religion, just love and devotion. My first ray focus was in full force, and at the heart of all my seeking was God.

From my late teens, I felt a need to protect the spiritual me, and so began to develop what I called Hats. I would personify who I thought I was meant to be for various situations. In doing so, I lost some of my authenticity. I did so much damage to myself by not allowing the authentic me to be present at every moment of every day. It wasn't until after the fourth initiation that I started to fully reclaim my authentic self, and in doing so, I went through the healing of self-rediscovery. I don't think I have totally reclaimed the original young me that had so much potential. I could blame the influence of others, but I have to take full responsibility for not supporting my true self.

I later realized that Sanat Kumara's lessons helped me cope with the vast energies I would encounter at the Ascended Masters' portal. The teaching from the Masters was, and is, constant. I have notebooks full of my understanding of the energetic self via them. Most of their teaching occurred in meditation in the form of a visual accompanied by a downloaded knowing. When seeing what they presented, I understood because of the download.

I feel it was at this time that I received my second crown chakra. This second crown chakra was placed there by the Masters for the Masters. This second crown chakra became an important part of my ongoing work with the Ascended Masters, for it meant they could work through me in clarity, unhindered by my lower vibration.

This was all pre-third initiation; it was after my third initiation in 2004 that life began to change. The initiations occur when the chakras have reached a certain percentage of maximum light. Think of total light in the chakras as potentially being one hundred percent light. The balance of light is karma. The third initiation occurs when the seven major chakras are all at sixty percent light and forty percent karma (darkness).

My third initiation was a mystical experience. It filled me with wonder and pain. I remember the pain vividly still. My initiation started with me feeling discombobulated for several weeks. I remember having pain in my chakras and being told ancient karma was being cleared.

On the evening of the initiation, my spine felt like a flame extending out through my crown chakra. I remember ironing and doing general household chores while dinner cooked and the children watched television. I remember sitting on the end of my bed wondering what was happening and deciding to meditate.

With my first breath, I was in an ascending pyramid. A man appeared before me. He had an orb above his head and a falcon beak on his forehead. He had wings that were at rest down his back; they looked like decoration. I went to bow to him, but he took my arm and stopped me, saying "No, don't do that. You are me and we are one." I saw coloured hieroglyphics in front of a flight of stairs. I asked his name. He said his name and wrote it in the air: *Ra-mun* (pronounced Ra-moon). He took me up to the apex of the pyramid and put a star tetrahedron into my heart chakra. This was so painful! When I came back to awareness, my heart chakra was still in pain. This pain came and went for several weeks. I discovered years later that Ra-mun was the Master of initiations.

About this time, I began to paint, guided by the Masters. Each new painting was a lesson in manifesting energy into the canvas. My second crown chakra was being utilized by the Masters, and we were learning how to work together.

When I started to paint with the Ascended Masters, Sanat Kumara came to me in meditation and taught me a new connection technique. I call it the Torus technique. It is a technique for connecting with the higher aspects of divine mind, sacred heart, and soul. This technique can be used in a group to manifest group consciousness and as a technique to connect to the Masters. I have used this technique many times a day since being taught by Sanat Kumara. It is truly a gift to us all. I have freely shared this technique, and it is available on my website at alphaimaging.co.nz

I was also working with a group of healers from all around the world to send healing to those who requested our free services. The Torus technique allowed us to work in healing unison. Service had become part of my daily life.

Despite all of this, I felt like I was walking in circles. I couldn't seem to find the path I was meant to be on. I felt frustrated. I could feel the push, but I didn't know the direction. In desperation, I sat in meditation one day and begged to be shown the path. Sanat Kumara came to me and gave me the Perfect Path technique. This technique was to guide me whenever I was in doubt as to my direction. I have used this technique so many times. Again, I freely share this technique on my website, alphaimaging.co.nz

In 2006, eighteen months after the third initiation, the fourth initiation occurred. For the initiation to have occurred, the light in my chakras was then at eighty percent, and the karma in my chakras had been reduced to twenty percent. In eighteen months, I had paid twenty percent more of my karma.

The fourth initiation was a very different initiation from the third. It occurred over two days in four parts. It began exactly at 10:49 am (eleven minutes to eleven o'clock) and ended at 11:11am, and then again in the evening at these same times. This happened four times in total. At each event, I saw a diamond shape above my crown chakra and then one in my third eye and heart chakra. Each event was concentrated on one of the bodies—astral, mental, emotional, and etheric bodies. Each body had many bands of energy around it. These bands were ties to past lives. With each event, these bands were released from the body. By the end of the fourth event, the bodies were bright light and the bands were gone. In this initiation, I wasn't aware of any Masters.

Then began a very long and hard climb to pay my last twenty percent of karma. My mantra for conduct was "God words, God thoughts, and God actions." To reflect my growing understanding of myself and others, I later changed my personal code of ethics to "heart-based words, heart-based thoughts, and heart-based action." This is still my code for living. I slip up, and I'm not perfect, but it is something I keep coming back to. When I do slip up, I used to be really hard on myself, until I realized that we create karma by not treating ourselves with love, respect, and kindness. My relationship with Self has changed since then. Loving Self is not easy. This karmic reality isn't easy. Karma creation is so very subtle that it is a miracle that any of us ever ascend at all.

Shortly after the fourth initiation, I met Waireti at a workshop that we both had attended. Waireti is my twin flame. I knew within myself that twin flames and soul mates can be of the same sex. Clear thinking tells us we have had both male and female past lives. Therefore, twin flames and soul mates must incarnate sometimes as the same sex.

Twin flames are the best and worst of relationships. The twin reflects back to us all that we need to work on within ourselves. Put ego into the mix, and the situation is fraught. But beneath all of this is a deep bond and a love that can't be denied. Most twin flame relationships don't last because the relationship isn't easy. Soul mates are the nice, easy relationships many dream of and seek. For Waireti and I, it is only with Ascension that our twin flame relationship has come into harmony.

In a soul mate relationship, the deep relationship is forged from repeated, loving past lives together. The twin flame relationship has nothing to do with the soul; rather, it is two Higher Selves that are the twin flames, and the lower selves are merely a reflection of that deeper and higher relationship. We can have many soul mates, but only one twin flame.

Waireti is very special, as she has dimensional sight. Dimensional sight is a term I made up to explain her ability to see *All*, the energetic world that exists around us and across dimensions and time. She sees the Ascended Masters, Angels, Archangels, Elohim, all the higher beings, and, sadly, all the lower beings that work at creating chaos in our world. She sometimes likens her sight to seeing multiple television screens.

The period between the fourth and fifth initiations was when I got to know the Ascended Masters in a deeper way. Mary Magdalene came to me and asked me to paint her portal painting. My art lessons from the Masters prepared me for this event. What I didn't know was that Mary Magdalene would paint her portal painting through me herself, utilizing my second crown chakra. In her painting, she created a doorway from her reality to ours. Through this doorway, her energy flows out to humanity twenty-four-seven. I showed the portal painting to Waireti, and she confirmed it was indeed the energy of Mary Magdalene. She also confirmed there was zero Verna Maruata energy in the painting. She confirmed this portal painting was a constant outpouring of Mary Magdalene's energy.

Jesus, St. Germain, and El Morya were next. With each new painting, I got Waireti to confirm these were portal paintings. I also got her to look and confirm what happened when I painted. She confirmed Verna was placed to one side, and the Masters came in and painted. They created their portals, not me.

After painting twenty-two Ascended Master portals, the Masters asked us to go on a road trip. We didn't know where we were going, only that they would guide us. We were told we would be gone for two weeks. After a few days, we found ourselves on a rough road in the Coromandel. At one point, Waireti was told to stop the car and walk along a rough, uneven path. After about ten minutes, she was told to stop and dig. There we found a large crystal; it was broken in two. Carrying one half each, we took it back to the car. We continued as guided. Sometimes we went up streams and into the bush and by rivers, always finding a stone energized by the Masters for whatever greater purpose they had.

One afternoon we were asked to enter a copse of trees. There I found some large, flat stones. I stood on them and Waireti said I disappeared. When I returned twenty minutes later, I knew we had to take the stones.

I had an awareness of what to do with the stones. There was no revelation, I just had an awareness. Digging them up revealed that the stones were like icebergs—only a small part of them was revealed. It looked like we would never be able to get these stones to the car, but Waireti told them to lighten and then picked them up, one by one, and carried them to the car. This was one of our many miracles.

All of these stones and, eventually, forty-four portal paintings formed the foundation in the physical for the Masters to begin the process of bringing the Ascended Masters' portal down to anchor into the Mother Earth. One hundred and eight Ascended Masters, Cosmic Masters, Devas, Archangels, and Elohim, working as a team, took three years to gradually descend the portal into the heavy vibration of this reality. Their purpose for doing this was to help humanity ascend.

Ten years since the creation of Mary Magdalene's portal painting, the Ascended Masters' portal is vast and complex. The Masters, Archangels, and Elohim work there daily with humanity. They have created oils that are little miracles in a bottle, oils that create change and assist with Ascension. They have manifested crystals in the portal, some for us, and some for those rare people the Masters select for us to pass them to. Waireti was constantly slipping across dimensions in the early days, so she asked the Masters for a form of grounding protection. They manifested a silver pendant for her to wear. One day we found the portal filled with gold leaf. They were obviously experimenting with various metals.

The events with the portal have been chronicled in my weekly diary posts on the Alpha Imaging website. You can read more about our adventures there, along with some of the Ascended Masters' teachings.

I look back and see how the Masters were quietly laying the stepping stones for my future work with them. They never at any time revealed the full picture of what was going to happen over the years.

There was never any grand revelation, just a quiet guidance. I feel if they had given us the big picture, ego would have stepped in. This way we just kept on as needed, and didn't give much thought to what was actually happening. People would praise me about the work I was doing, and I would look blankly at them. I felt nothing, and this is still the case. Waireti and I look at each other sometimes and ask each other, "Did they get the right people?" We feel quite detached from all that has happened and now exists.

Despite what was happening in our external world, the journey within became the most important focus of all as I discovered the Sacred Heart within, and then the Holy Heart beyond that. The Holy Heart is the Holy of Holies within; it is where the Higher Self will eventually reside within you after the seventh initiation.

The fifth initiation was a momentous occasion. It meant my chakras were one hundred percent light and there was no karma remaining in any of the chakras. I was released from the cycle of rebirth. My last life on Earth had been lived. It took more than eighteen thousand lives to achieve this goal, but finally, my self-created karma was paid. My ties with the Mother Earth were severed at the initiation. I was no longer of the Mother; I was no longer one of those she held within her, life after life. Instead, I graduated to the vast and cosmic world of the Father. The actual process of the initiation is detailed on the Alpha Imaging website.

But life went on. There was no great change in my life. My work with the Ascended Masters continued. My meditations in the Sacred Heart and Holy Heart continued. The website grew, and the type of healings we offered with the Ascended Masters became more Ascension focused, as did the products.

I thought this was the end of my Ascension, as my light was at full capacity within the chakras, but this wasn't the case. With the Ascended Masters, we are always learning. It became clear the initiations were continuing and Ascension was continuing. I was unsure as to what might occur next, but we kept on. We were beginning to feel like Ascension explorers. I continued to learn from the Ascended Masters. Much of what I learned I shared on the website in articles and the weekly diary.

Ascension, we learned, was now about perfecting the lower self; the conquering of fears; the letting go of old patterns of thought, speech, and actions that were not part of our highest good; the payment of karma for others; and the journey of the Higher Self into form, from its safe and beautiful place of light into the dark and heavy world we inhabit. Higher Self was preparing to be the Master in body. My Higher Self was also planning for His continued Ascension, as he could ascend in a clearer and faster way while in body than out of body. The Ascending Higher Selves were preparing to join the Ascended Masters in their service to humanity.

A year after the fifth initiation, I passed the sixth. This was when my Higher Self started to descend into form. This was a twenty-month process. Each month, Waireti recorded the percentage descent of Higher Self. It was a slow process. We weren't alone though—others we were working with were ascending with us. We were becoming an Ascension family. We continued to clear the karma of others; most often it was unwanted and unexpected. This clearing happened in our physical bodies, and it could be uncomfortable and painful.

Devotion to my Higher Self in the Holy Heart and the letting go of so much of my lower self became a daily process. My previous devotion to my external God had matured to the devotion to my inner god, my Higher Self. The esoteric writings were right—the pathway was an inner path. All pathways must converge to this one single route, regardless of beliefs and doctrine. For the pathway of Sacred Heart, Holy Heart, and beyond is the only route to Ascension after the fifth initiation.

There are so many possible modalities for Ascension, but there is only one way to ascend. There is only one pathway from the karmic darkness into the light, and that is the path of Self. We all must pay our karma until the point that there is no karma left, and we leave the cycle of rebirth with perfected, light-filled chakras. From there we follow the path of the Sacred Heart to the Holy Heart, and to our own Higher Self, our own personal god. For our Higher Self has an Ascension journey of its own—it is ascending into Christ Light. This is a process beyond our physical existence, and one we are not a part of. For the life of the Higher Self continues after we return home to our source, our Higher Self.

At the sixth initiation, I discovered my Higher Self was male. This came as a complete shock, as I had been connected with whom I had thought was my female Higher Self, Pallas Athena, up until then—I had confused an encounter with her, way back before the third initiation, for my Higher Self. I had slipped up; I hadn't practiced discernment. I had maintained that misunderstanding for so many years, it was embarrassing. How dejected my true Higher Self must have felt. I caution everyone to not assume they know their Higher Self until they pass the sixth initiation. I have learned that the Higher Self isn't even particularly interested in us, as they are overseeing probably twelve to twenty-seven more souls across dimensions; we are merely one of those. The Higher Self places us in the keeping of the Ascended Masters until such time as they can work on their personal Ascension through one of their souls.

You might remember that, back at the start of my story, I told you my birth rays were 1-1-3-1-1. At the sixth initiation, all the birth rays are removed. These rays are replaced with the single ray of the Higher Self. My Higher Self is a Master of the second ray, the yellow ray of Wisdom and Joy. All my rays turned to his specific second ray yellow, which is a soft pale yellow. My rays are now 2-2-2-2-2. When the change of rays occurred, this was a time of mourning for me. Not only was I saying goodbye to El Morya and Kuan Yin, as they now stepped back, but I was also losing much of what had defined me as a first-ray soul. The second ray, in contrast, is a ray of Lightness of Being. All the Masters on the second ray are approachable, friendly, and wise. This is what my Higher Self is like. I don't see myself fitting in at all; I love my old first-ray self. But change occurs slowly as I let go of who I was and open myself up to change.

Now, having passed the seventh initiation, my Higher Self resides fully in my Holy Heart. My Higher Self is a Master in my body. I am still the lower self. I still am me in many ways. I have negative thoughts still, I am not perfect. My body is still imperfect. My Higher Self has descended into this dark world we live in with two purposes: to help humanity ascend and to ascend himself.

You have seen my journey from my own darkness into a light greater than I imagined.

Ascension continues for me and humanity, just as it continues for you.

January, 2019

Note; As of August, 2019, one hundred and ten people have passed the sixth initiation and thirty-eight have passed the seventh initiation through the Ascended Masters portal. Those of us who have passed the seventh initiation work in groups to help humanity in so many ways. We are serving with our Higher Selves and the Ascended Masters.

Conclusion

The opportunity to achieve Ascension in your lifetime has never been greater than now. All of the storytellers here are way-showers for the rapid Ascension path now available to everyone. By telling our stories about our Ascension paths and our spiritual journeys, we are helping others to see the possibility of Ascension for themselves.

We have been blessed by having our project over-lighted by Ganesh, a Cosmic Master on the fifth ray of Healing, Knowledge, and Personal Truth. Ganesh is not just the "remover of obstacles" (although we appreciate His role here in smoothing the path for this book to come to fruition). He is also the only Master who shows the physical evidence of flaws and the masks we wear to portray a better picture of ourselves. The writers here all wrote openly about some of the more difficult and vulnerable parts of their lives, and as you have read, some have faced very difficult circumstances. They unmasked themselves for you. They wanted to show you that their life journeys, however tough, have been perfect for the fulfillment of their destinies.

As we continue to ascend, we gather to participate with others at a higher level of service to the world and its inhabitants. This work is accomplished through group Torus meditation work. The Torus groups are dedicated to various causes that arise in current events

CONCLUSION

around the world. The Elohim, Cosmic and Ascended Masters, Archangels, Devas and our Higher Selves work through us to help humanity in myriad ways.

We hope that the effects of this work will help to create positive change worldwide. It is inevitable that old structures and systems that perpetuate separation, disparity, and inequality will crumble and be replaced with new, more humanistic models of thinking and acting: in government, in the classroom, in health care, in economies, in politics, and so on. There will hopefully be an emphasis on the recognition of the inherent worth of all life and the rights for all to live in peace, harmony, love, and abundance. No longer will it be acceptable for one to be simply serving the self through satisfying the ego demands, needs, and wants. As we grow into our true spiritual nature, we will want to act in much more expansive and open-hearted ways. We will participate in cooperative ventures for the benefit of all. We will have respect for all life.

Ascension does not come with a guarantee that the rest of one's life will be entirely free of problems and difficulties. We all have to live and sustain ourselves as we go through life. But it will guarantee that you have cleared your karma; it will provide you with an opportunity to leave the cycle of rebirth with its long history of past lives, each of which generally begins without memory of one's purpose. And it will give you the opportunity to choose to live authentically with your Higher Self and to grow into the best version of yourself. You will be of service to life using your gifts and talents. Furthermore, you will have expanded spiritually in the most phenomenal way while living on earth.

The opportunity for rapid Ascension exists now. We encourage you to take up the challenge and direct your efforts to your Ascension process. The effects of your efforts aren't just personal. All life in our cosmos and beyond will experience the positive ripple of your expansion efforts. Do this for the love of self and all of life.

Our hope is that Ascension has been demystified for you and presented as achievable for everyone. We have presented our understanding of what has transpired for us. Although there is limited human comprehension of the enormity of this experience, there was an attempt here to capture in words our personal experiences of Ascension.

It may sound like an achievement model, with its higher numbers equating to higher levels, but it isn't about seeking a diploma or certification in any earthly sense. There is a Grace and Love that grants this opportunity openly to all who seek it.

There was a time when this was rarely possible for humans to achieve. Now it is open to everyone and you can ascend while still living in human form, and be here in great service to humanity. This is a new paradigm.

Ascension is a possibility for you in these modern times. Tap into the unlimited support available from the Ascended Masters and take this journey. And let your heart guide you on your perfect path.

Blessings from all of us to all of you.

CPSIA information can be obtained
at www.ICGtesting.com
Printed in the USA
FSHW011331271219
65518FS